Doing "Women's Work"

RESEARCH ON MEN AND MASCULINITIES SERIES

Series Editor:
MICHAEL S. KIMMEL, SUNY Stony Brook

Contemporary research on men and masculinity, informed by recent feminist thought and intellectual breakthroughs of women's studies and the women's movement, treats masculinity not as a normative referent but as a problematic gender construct. This series of interdisciplinary, edited volumes attempts to understand men and masculinity through this lens, providing a comprehensive understanding of gender and gender relationships in the contemporary world. Published in cooperation with the Men's Studies Association, a Task Group of the National Organization for Men Against Sexism.

Volumes in this Series

Doing "Women's Work"
Men in Nontraditional Occupations

Edited by Christine L. Williams

SAGE Publications
International Educational and Professional Publisher
Newbury Park   London   New Delhi

For information address:

 SAGE Publications, Inc.
2455 Teller Road
Newbury Park, California 91320

SAGE Publications Ltd.
6 Bonhill Street
London EC2A 4PU
United Kingdom

SAGE Publications India Pvt. Ltd.
M-32 Market
Greater Kailash I
New Delhi 110 048 India

Printed in the United States of America

Library of Congress Cataloging-in-Publication Data

Doing "women's work": men in nontraditional occupations / edited by
Christine L. Williams.
        p. cm.—(Research on men and masculinity series ; 3)
    Includes bibliographical references and index.
    ISBN 0-8039-5304-6 (cloth).—ISBN 0-8039-5305-4 (pbk.)
    1. Sex role in the work environment. 2. Sex discrimination
against men. 3. Sex discrimination in employment. 4. Stereotype
(Psychology) I. Williams, Christine L., 1959-   . II. Series.
HD6060.6.D65   1993
305.33—dc20
                                                              93-25055
                                                                   CIP

94 95 96 10 9 8 7 6 5 4 3 2

Sage Production Editor: Megan M. McCue

Contents

Acknowledgments

I am grateful to several people for their help in putting this book together. Michael Kimmel came up with the idea to produce this volume, and he has been a very supportive and instructive series editor. Mitch Allen, my editor at Sage, has been enthusiastic and helpful throughout the process.

I also extend my deepest thanks to my colleagues who served as reviewers: Dana Britton, Sam Cohn, Susan Marshall, Livia Pohlman, Art Sakamoto, Teresa Sullivan, and Debra Umberson. Their critical comments and suggestions were extremely useful in developing the papers that appear in this volume.

Finally, I am indebted to the contributors who devoted their time to this project. They displayed great professionalism and patience, making the process both enlightening and enjoyable for me.

Foreword

When I was a graduate student, I earned extra money teaching at a local nursery school. I was the only male teacher in the school, and I recall distinctly the reaction of one of the childrens' parents to my presence on the first day of school. Brad was a quiet boy, shy and very sweet, who loved painting on the easels we had set up inside the classroom. The other boys would often enter school by tearing through the indoor play areas and go right for the gross motor areas we had set up outside. When Brad's parents saw me, their eyes lit up and they were overjoyed. "A male teacher," they sighed with relief. "Please get Brad away from the painting and out to the yard to play with the truck and the other boys," they pleaded. Their fear about the meaning of Brad's gender nonconformity was palpable, and I wondered if we would collaborate in the discouragement of a future artist. Interestingly, however, the fact that I was a man doing "women's work" did not dissuade them from their belief that I could rescue their son from a life of gender nonconformity.

A few years later, I was again confronted with these issues. I appeared in a television documentary about the ways men's roles were changing. One of the men interviewed was a nurse, whose mother was somewhat embarrassed about her son's occupation. When asked what her son did for a living, she would respond—without pausing for breath—"My son's a nurse and he's not gay."

I've been wrestling with similar issues ever since I undertook a documentary history of "pro-feminist" men in the United States (published in 1992 as *Against the Tide: Pro-Feminist Men in the United States, 1776-1990*). After all, aren't men who support women's equality actually men who are doing "women's work," agitating for gender equality in the public and private spheres? And the men whose work I documented had always faced questions about their manhood, from Frederick Douglass, who was branded a "political hermaphrodite" and an "Aunt Nancy Man" to contemporary men who are decried as "wimps" by those who think that support for women indicates insufficient gender identity.

I was reminded of these issues when I read Christine Williams's excellent book, *Gender Differences at Work* (1989), and I invited her to assemble the best research available in the social sciences that concerns itself with the question of gender nonconformity in occupations. Now, I am delighted to introduce *Doing "Women's Work": Men in Nontraditional Occupations* into the Sage Series on Men and Masculinities, because I believe that it presents a challenging set of articles that raise the issues of gender and the workplace in very significant ways.

Interestingly, the articles in this book suggest that crossing over—men doing "women's work"—cuts both ways. On the one hand, there are significant costs for the men, as their manhood and sexuality are often questioned as a result of occupational choices. On the other hand, there are often significant gains that they also receive, such as higher wages than women doing the same work. The articles in this book provide a nuanced and complex understanding of the ways in which occupations, as well as individuals, are gendered.

MICHAEL S. KIMMEL
Series Editor

1

Introduction

CHRISTINE L. WILLIAMS

In most industrialized countries of the world, women are about as likely as men are to work in the paid labor force. Women make up more than 40% of the labor force in the United States, Canada, most countries of Europe, and Australia. But despite their growing representation among paid workers, only rarely do women work alongside men, performing the same tasks and functions in the same industries. Most jobs are very clearly divided into "men's work" and "women's work." In the United States, for example, more than half of all men or women would have to change major job categories in order to equalize the number of men and women in all jobs (Reskin & Hartmann, 1986). In Sweden, which has the highest rate of women's paid labor force participation in the world, sex segregation is even more extreme (Borchorst & Siim, 1987).

Occupational sex segregation is a major social problem for working women. Often it is credited with sustaining, if not causing the wage gap, the substantial difference in the salaries paid to full-time men and women workers. Women earn less than men in every country, largely because they are concentrated in "female" jobs that pay less than "male" jobs. Female jobs also tend to be less prestigious and autonomous than male jobs. It is no wonder, then, that feminists have worked hard to break down the barriers of segregation and encourage more women to enter traditionally defined male jobs.

Sociologists too have focused their analyses of occupational segregation on women's exclusion from predominately male jobs. Books have been written on practically every male-dominated occupation—from medicine and law to business management and the trades—to

1

determine what keeps women out of these fields, and to document the ongoing discrimination suffered by the few women who manage to break through the barriers. Indeed, most of what we know about occupational segregation is based on these studies of women's experiences in male jobs (e.g., Epstein, 1981; Kanter, 1977; Reskin & Roos, 1990; Stiehm, 1989).

But looking at segregation as something that happens only to women gives us only a partial picture. Occupational sex segregation is a two-way street: It is just as important to understand what keeps men out of female jobs as it is to understand what keeps women out of male jobs. And the fact is that men are even less likely than women to aspire to and work in gender-atypical jobs. While the proportions of women in several male-dominated jobs have dramatically increased over the past 20 years, predominately female jobs have changed their sex compositions very little, if at all (Jacobs, 1989; Reskin & Roos, 1990).

Yet very few people have examined why men are vastly underrepresented in traditionally female jobs, and what happens to the few men who do "cross over." This collection of essays is one of the first attempts to systematically examine these questions. It brings together research from a variety of disciplines to document and explain the social and economic forces that sustain the exclusion of men from predominantly female jobs.

Bringing men into our analysis of segregation has the potential to transform our sociological understanding of how gender operates in the work world. For too long, the study of occupations has been conducted with a gender-neutral framework. Sociologists and economists typically have assumed that capitalism creates occupational slots, indifferent to who fills what positions. Conservative theorists have argued that because men and women are socialized differently, they are suited to different types of work, hence women predominate in the more nurturing, expressive jobs, whereas men are concentrated in jobs that require more technical proficiency and decision-making ability (e.g., Parsons & Bales, 1955; Simpson & Simpson, 1969). Other, more radical theorists have claimed that patriarchy, rather than socialization, accounts for women's concentration in lesser-paying and lower status jobs (e.g., Eisenstein, 1979; Hartmann, 1976).

Both of these positions are inadequate because, as several of the essays in this volume show, occupations are structured with the particular gender of the laborer in mind. In other words, the positions themselves are not gender-neutral but have built into them assumptions about the kind of workers likely to be employed in them (Acker, 1990, 1992; Baron, 1991).

One of the clearest examples of this "gendering" of occupations is the medical division of labor between doctors and nurses. Prior to this modern division, both men and women performed diagnostic, curative techniques as well as caregiving functions (although on very different clienteles). Separating these functions involved barring women from schools of medicine, and excluding men from nursing programs. In other words, assumptions about gender were built into the elaboration of these two separate professions. Similar developments occurred in the history of secretarial work, teaching, retail trade, and certain types of factory work: Jobs were developed for women, based on cultural assumptions of women's nature and their proper place in society (Baron, 1991; Davies, 1982; Kessler-Harris, 1990; Reverby, 1987; Vicinus, 1985).

The man who crosses over into a female-dominated occupation upsets these gender assumptions embedded in the work. Almost immediately, he is suspected of not being a "real man": There must be something wrong with him ("Is he gay? Effeminate? Lazy?") for him to be interested in this kind of work. If these popular prejudices are not enough to push him out of his occupation, they will certainly affect how he manages his gender identity on a daily basis. Men in these occupations often emphasize their masculinity and attempt to distance themselves from their female colleagues, as a way to legitimize their working in female jobs (Williams, 1989).

Women who "cross over" are also subject to suspicions that they are not "real women," but they are far more constrained in how they respond to these prejudices (Spencer & Podmore, 1987). Emphasizing their femininity (whatever that may mean) will have limited benefit for women in an occupational structure defined and controlled by men. But for men in women's jobs, masculinity can be a boon, because qualities associated with men are more highly regarded than those associated with women, even in predominantly female jobs. This is partly because men tend to monopolize positions of power in these occupations, and they can make decisions about employees that favor other men. But also, this fact reflects a widespread cultural prejudice that men are simply better than women. Thus, men are rewarded for emphasizing their difference from women; women are typically penalized for any difference they (willingly or not) represent from men.

The essays in this collection document the consequences of our societal preference for men: The men who work in predominantly female occupations receive greater pay and benefits than their female counterparts. But the essays also show that despite this privileged status, it is still quite rare for men to cross over into these jobs, and the few men who do cross over usually don't stay very long. While popular prejudices might account for why some men leave these jobs, many leave after a short period of time to take jobs that are more "appropriate" for men. In most cases, this will mean an increase in pay and prestige, as jobs that are predominantly male are more highly rewarded than those that are predominantly female.

Looking at occupations as gendered institutions can help us make sense of why so few men work in nontraditional jobs, and why those who do are generally so successful. Research has shown that women cannot simply "fill in" slots intended for male workers; this collection also shows that men cannot simply "fill in" slots intended for women. People do not check their gender at the factory gates or office door; whether they are men or women will greatly affect how they are treated in the workplace. Occupations are not gender-neutral. As several of these essays indicate, jobs are transformed when the gender of the worker changes.

In addition to broadening our understanding of the process of occupational sex segregation, the study of men working in predominantly female jobs also informs the more overtly political project of ending segregation. As I have already mentioned, most of the energy devoted to breaking down segregation has focused on getting women into male-dominated fields. Young women today are being told that to obtain decent salaries and respectability, they need to take classes in mathematics and science, and eventually enter "men's jobs." This advice is rarely accompanied by encouragement to young men to enter "women's jobs." But, clearly, eliminating segregation would require equalizing the proportion of men and women in all jobs, not just the jobs that are currently male-dominated. Of course, this is all very complicated, because once men enter female-dominated jobs, they tend to rise to the top, reproducing gender hierarchy within jobs. So ending segregation is no simple matter. But if we do not work to change the gender composition of all jobs—which means both encouraging women to be more like men and encouraging men to be more like women—we run the risk of reproducing the sexist devaluation of everything female/feminine, making men the ultimate measure of success.

The essays in this collection all indicate just how difficult it will be to get men into predominantly female jobs. In "Across the Great Divide,"

Harriet Bradley examines the very limited circumstances under which men have historically crossed over into female-dominated jobs. She points out that there are far more examples of occupations changing from male to female than from female to male. A radical transformation in female jobs is usually necessary before men are attracted to them in any great number. This is a recurring theme throughout many of the essays: Crossing over does not necessarily undermine the system of occupational segregation, or the sexism that underlies it. Rather, as Bradley indicates, the large-scale movement of men or women into gender-atypical occupations is typically produced by some crisis or industrial change that leaves the system of gender hierarchy intact.

Men's reluctance to enter female-dominated jobs is usually attributed to their lesser pay. Paula England and Melissa Herbert assess the claim that men who work in predominantly female jobs earn less than those employed in more traditional lines of work. They find that there is indeed an economic penalty suffered by both men and women for working in jobs that employ mostly women, and that men suffer a greater wage loss than women (compared to what they could be making in male jobs). The wage disparity between men's and women's work is not due to characteristics intrinsic to female-dominated work. Rather, they conclude that the economic difference in pay is due to the cultural devaluation of women—and overvaluation of men. In their view, achieving economic equality between men and women would require a radical reassessment of the cultural value placed on "women's work," which is precisely the political strategy endorsed by the "comparable worth" movement.

The next two essays examine the careers of men who aspire to and enter predominately female occupations. Jerry Jacobs applies his concept of "revolving doors" to analyze the mobility patterns of men into and out of female-dominated jobs. His research demonstrates that, while very few men aspire to or work in female jobs, the few that do express interest in pursuing these jobs, or actually enter them, do not stay very long. He suggests that a system of lifelong social control produces a revolving door for those men who try to cross over: They are typically channeled and rechanneled out of these jobs, and into jobs that are more male-dominated.

L. Susan Williams and Wayne J. Villemez look closely at the characteristics of men who work in female-dominated jobs. They found that while some men aspired to these jobs, others entered these jobs through a "trap door": They intended to pursue more traditional male careers but for some reason they ended up in predominantly female jobs. Also, like Jacobs, Williams and Villemez note that the few men who do cross over rarely stay very long: Some men find they are barred from obtaining female jobs, despite their aspirations; others are escalated to better jobs after only a brief tenure in nontraditional areas of work. Their study provides a nuanced view of how the occupational structure operates in a gendered way to restrict individual choice.

Kaisa Kauppinen-Toropainen and Johanna Lammi provide a comparative perspective by examining case studies of men in female jobs in the Nordic countries. Their research confirms that occupational sex segregation is indeed a cross-cultural phenomenon, although the specific occupations labeled male or female can and do vary. In general, though, those occupations that involve direct personal caretaking (particularly of people who are either very young or very old) tend to be female-dominated. These jobs also tend to be lesser paid, of lower status, and less autonomous than jobs that are more traditionally held by men. Kauppinen-Toropainen and Lammi review several studies on the reasons for men's reluctance to enter traditionally female jobs, and the various satisfactions and dissatisfactions men experience while working in selected female jobs.

These first five essays provide the social, economic, and cultural context for understanding men's experiences in nontraditional occupations. The essays that follow document the actual experiences of men in four specific female-dominated occupations: elementary school teaching, secretarial work, unpaid elder care, and striptease dancing. These case studies provide rich accounts of the dynamic ways that gender differences are reproduced at work, and how men's advantages in the workplace are sustained even when they cross over. Men use various strategies to maintain their masculinity in these occupations, often transforming the work in the process.

Jim Allan discusses the advantages and disadvantages that accrue to men in elementary school teaching, focusing on hiring decisions. He shows that even though there is a preference for hiring men teachers in primary grades, this can place men in an untenable situation vis-à-vis their male supervisors and female colleagues: While their male bosses expect them to engage in male bonding activities with them, this sort of behavior places them at odds with their female colleagues. Similarly, if male teachers ally themselves with the women teachers, they are perceived as a threat by the men in charge. Allan argues that men must negotiate the meaning of their masculinity in the workplace, navigating between the extremes represented by others' expectations of them. He suggests that leaving the occupation is one of the ways that men respond to these conflicting demands, which obviously leaves the gendered structure of the occupation intact.

Rosemary Pringle examines additional ways that occupations engender differences in male and female employees. Her study of male secretaries shows that even when men and women are employed to do the same tasks, they are rarely categorized together as sharing the same occupation. However, in the few instances she did encounter of men categorized as secretaries, she found that they redefined their work to accommodate their sense of maleness. In her view, occupational integration holds very little promise for challenging gender inequality. Occupational sex segregation is a symptom of men's desire to differentiate from women and dominate them, and it is this deeper problem that must be addressed before workplace equality between men and women can be achieved.

The next essay, by Jeffrey Applegate and Lenard Kaye, examines an unpaid female occupation: caring for the elderly. Drawing on interviews with men who have primary responsibility for caring for their elderly relatives, Applegate and Kaye show that men can and do develop the skills and personality traits normally associated with women. Nevertheless, their research indicates that the ideology of masculinity remains viable, despite this apparent transformation in the men. That is, even though these men are engaged in nurturing and expressive tasks, they do not question the traditional division between male and female roles. Their study indicates that the system of gender differentiation is apparently resilient to the kind of work men and women actually perform, suggesting once again that occupational integration will not solve the problem of gender inequality.

The final essay, by Richard Tewksbury, examines an underground occupation, striptease dancing. Tewksbury studied four all-male stripping troupes who perform for male audiences. Using a dramaturgical approach, he argues that when men perform this traditionally female role, the role is transformed—not the men. New elements of masculinity are incorporated into the role that enable men to preserve a sense of themselves as masculine and powerful.

Taken as a group, the essays in this collection do not bode well for the future of gender equality. They convince me that occupational integration is no panacea to the economic problems of women. Without addressing the underlying problem—our cultural overvaluation of men and devaluation of women—gender inequality will persist despite the entry of men and women into gender-atypical occupations.

There is no question that men can do the work usually assigned to women. The basic problem, and the challenge for those interested in gender equality, is to get men to want to do this work alongside women, without fear or derision. Of course, as long as women's work pays less and is less prestigious than men's work, even those men committed to gender equity are unlikely to even consider crossing over. The essays in this collection demonstrate how entrenched occupational segregation is, and how far we have to go before men and women achieve true economic equality.

References

Acker, J. (1990). Hierarchies, jobs, bodies: A theory of gendered organizations. *Gender & Society, 4*, 139-158.

Acker, J. (1992). From sex roles to gendered institutions. *Contemporary Sociology, 21*, 565-569.

Baron, A. (1991). Gender and labor history: Learning from the past, looking to the future. In A. Baron (Ed.), *Work engendered: Toward a new history of American labor* (pp. 1-46). Ithaca, NY: Cornell University Press.

Borchorst, A., & Siim, B. (1987). Women and the advanced welfare state—A new kind of patriarchal power? In A. Showstack-Sassoon (Ed.), *Women and the state* (pp. 128-157). London: Hutchinson.

Davies, M. (1982). *Woman's place is at the typewriter: Office work and office workers, 1870-1930.* Philadelphia: Temple University Press.

Eisenstein, Z. (1979). *Capitalist patriarchy and the case for socialist feminism.* New York: Monthly Review Press.

Epstein, C. F. (1981). *Women in law.* New York: Basic Books.

Hartmann, H. (1976, Spring). Capitalism, patriarchy, and job segregation by sex. *Signs, 1*(3), 137-169.

Jacobs, J. A. (1989). *Revolving doors: Sex segregation and women's careers.* Palo Alto, CA: Stanford University Press.

Kanter, R. M. (1977). *Men and women of the corporation.* New York: Basic Books.

Kessler-Harris, A. (1990). *A woman's wage: Historical meanings and social consequences.* Lexington: University of Kentucky Press.

Parsons, T., & Bales, R. (1955). *Family: Socialization and interaction process.* Glencoe, IL: Free Press.

Reskin, B., & Hartmann, H. (1986). *Women's work, men's work: Sex segregation on the job.* Washington, DC: National Academy Press.

Reskin, B., & Roos, P. (1990). *Job queues, gender queues: Explaining women's inroads into male occupations.* Philadelphia: Temple University Press.

Reverby, S. M. (1987). *Ordered to care: The dilemma of American nursing, 1850-1945.* Cambridge: Cambridge University Press.

Simpson, R. L., & Simpson, I. H. (1969). Women and bureaucracy in the semi-professions. In A. Etzioni (Ed.), *The semi-professions and their organization,* (pp. 196-265). New York: Free Press.

Spencer, A., & Podmore, D. (1987). *In a man's world: Essays on women in male-dominated professions.* London & New York: Tavistock.

Stiehm, J. H. (1989). *Arms and the enlisted woman.* Philadelphia: Temple University Press.

Vicinus, M. (1985). *Independent women: Work and community for single women, 1850-1920.* Chicago: University of Chicago Press.

Williams, C. L. (1989). *Gender differences at work.* Berkeley: University of California Press.

2

Across the Great Divide

The Entry of Men Into "Women's Jobs"

HARRIET BRADLEY

Feminist scholarship has taken the concept of the sexual division of labor to be a central category in the understanding of gender relations and of power disparities between women and men. A now weighty body of research, carried out by sociologists, historians, and anthropologists, has uncovered the processes by which social tasks become sex-typed (assigned as work suitable either for men or for women) and the ways in which sex-typing and the segregation of women and men in employment are maintained. These studies have revealed not only how variable and diverse the sexual division of labor has been between different societies, cultures, and epochs, but also how widespread and pervasive gender segregation is.

In particular, the impact of industrialization on jobs has been seen to produce a new pattern of sex-typing, which, despite national variations, is replicated in most advanced industrial nations of the First World: concentration of men in heavy industry and craft production; the use of women in repetitive semiskilled or unskilled factory work, such as electrical and electronic assembly; the dominance of men in the traditional professions, such as law and medicine, and the clustering of women in the semiprofessions such as nursing and school teaching; the growth of women's employment in low-paid service work in the postwar period, especially in clerical work and catering; men's near-monopoly of top managerial positions in most areas of the economy. Some commentators (for example, Boserup, 1970; Bradley, 1989; Lown, 1990) have suggested that the processes of industrial capitalist development have served to rigidify the structure of job segregation by sex, in comparison with preindustrial societies; and Hakim's renowned statistical study (1979) suggested that structures of both horizontal segregation (clustering of women and men in different occupations) and vertical segregation (concentration of men in the top posts in each occupation) have remained basically constant over most of this century.

Study of gender segregation has encouraged research interest in the circumstances in which women move into jobs previously designated as male. This process has been investigated in a number of historical and contemporary studies (for example, Cockburn, 1985; Holcombe, 1973; Matthaei, 1982; Walby, 1986; Zimmeck, 1986). This has been linked to current perception of a "feminization" of the work force in many industrial societies in the past two decades, as a result of changes in national economies and in the global structure of capitalism (Jenson, Hagen, & Reddy, 1988). It is argued that in America these decades have seen a push of women into traditionally male areas (Reskin & Roos, 1990), perhaps in part because of feminist pressure. But much less attention has been paid to the movement of men into women's jobs.

This may partly be because such cases are comparatively rare; it also reflects the evolution of contemporary study of gender, which started as an attempt to rediscover the lost histories and experiences of women. This original "Women's Studies" approach has expanded its scope to include an understanding of how the experiences of both sexes are inextricably linked together; and there has also been a move to reinterpret male experiences and generate new approaches to the study of men and masculinities, which have been vigorously pursued in both Britain and America under the rubric of "Men's Studies." The way ideas of masculinity are bound up with the breadwinner role and linked to certain forms of employment, along with the threats to masculinity brought by unemployment and the decline of traditional heavy industry, have been emergent themes of such studies (see, among many others, Brittan, 1989; Connell, 1987; Morgan, 1992).

In this chapter, I want to provide some general discussion of how men cross over into jobs sex-typed as female, as a background to the case studies of masculinization that follow. The chapter presents a typology of three characteristic patterns of male entry into women's work, derived from a survey of research into past cases in Britain and the United States, where this process has occurred. Some of these cases are given as examples to illustrate each of the three modes of entry. On the basis of these, I then seek to identify the key factors that encourage men to enter women's jobs and give some thought to what the implications are for likely future development.

Before setting out the typology, it is necessary briefly to review the factors that serve to uphold the rigidity of the sexual division of labor, and then to consider the circumstances in which this rigidity breaks down so that jobs either lose their gender associations or are reassigned to the opposite sex. For this purpose I return to the literature on sex segregation, which, as I have indicated above, has mostly been oriented to the study of women's jobs and of feminization.

Divided Work: The Origins and Maintenance of Sex-Typing in Employment

Early accounts of gender segregation at work (for example, Baker, 1964; Clark, 1982; Holcombe, 1973; Oakley, 1976) tended to focus on the impact of capitalist industrialization on the sexual division of labor. Capitalists were seen to benefit from gender segregation, which enabled them to set lower rates of pay for women's work. Jobs were often redesigned with women in mind: sometimes through the use of technological innovation, sometimes by subdividing existing jobs into several tasks and assigning more routinized and less responsible tasks to women. As well as cutting labor costs, such strategic decisions by capitalist employers served to fragment the labor force and worked against the development of a unified trade union movement. Women were preferred in certain jobs not simply because of the cheapness of their labor but because they were considered more docile and biddable, less likely to resist efforts toward intensified work and to complain about poor conditions and rewards.

More recent work, however, has been based firmly on the premise that the sexual division of labor predated capitalist industrialism. Dual systems theory suggests that capitalist and patriarchal motivations entwined together to produce the current structure of sex-typed jobs (Hartmann, 1976; Walby, 1986). Ortner (1974), like other feminist anthropologists, has argued that because of male social dominance, whatever activities are undertaken by men receive the highest social evaluation. Once tasks have been defined as having high status, men have the power to organize together to monopolize them and exclude women from them. At the same time whatever work is done by women tends to be devalued (be it housework or sewing or nursing), in the sense of both receiving lower economic rewards and holding lower social prestige. As many feminists have argued, in the industrial epoch this has been accomplished partly by seeing skills associated with female tasks, such as those listed above, as "natural"; thus the skills acquired by women slide into invisibility while skills required in "male" tasks are brought to the foreground by formal training procedures, such as university degrees or apprenticeships. Through such processes a hierarchical division of labor emerges and is perpetuated by men's activities to defend it. In the nineteenth century, male professional bodies and trade unions played an important role in keeping women out of jobs designated as male specializations and pushing them into female ghettos.

Witz (1992) has recently suggested that the role of trade unions in promoting sex segregation has been exaggerated by Hartmann and Walby. She bases this argument on the relative weakness of nineteenth-century unions and the small percentage of the work force that belonged to them. However, this overlooks the extent to which the ideas and aspirations of male trade unionists corresponded to the ideas held by most men in Victorian society, including capitalist employers. Ideologies and discourses of gender have always had a crucial role in promoting and sustaining structural divisions of gender. In preindustrial societies, tradition and religion provided the framework for views about the suitability of tasks for women or for men. The work of Hall (1979) and others has shown how religion continued to play a crucial part after industrialization in formulating the new "domestic ideology," which justified the assignment of women to homemaking, or to consonant caring tasks if they were to be allowed to work outside the home. This was backed up by medical and scientific discourses that portrayed women as dominated by their biology in a way that men were not, and as being therefore intrinsically less rational and less suited for intellectually demanding or technological work. Such views, although to some extent challenged by nineteenth-century feminists, provided the intellectual backing for many of the campaigns to keep women out of certain types of work, ranging from medical practice to agricultural fieldwork. Acceptance of these ideas by many men (and women) provided the basis for a collusion between male employers and male unionists, however limited the unionists' power might have been. I have suggested elsewhere (Bradley, 1989) that such a collusion evolved toward the end of the nineteenth century and helped consolidate the pattern of sex-typing that has persisted fairly undisturbed throughout the twentieth century in Britain and America (Hakim, 1979; Mallier & Rosser, 1987).

Structural forces (the capitalist drive for accumulation, the hierarchies that perpetuate male social dominance) have, I am arguing, come together with ideologies and discourses of femininity and masculinity to produce an effect of gendering within the employment sphere. Some of the most illuminating work on this process of gendering has come from Cynthia Cockburn (1983, 1985, 1991). Both jobs and workplaces, she argues, are gendered. Jobs, old and new, are not seen as neutral but are conceptualized in terms of their suitability for either sex, with notions of male technical superiority having a particular salience in sex-typing. Cultures that develop in workplaces among work groups are often single-sex and serve to police the boundaries between female and male jobs. Studies such as Cockburn's suggest that many workers prefer to work only with their own sex, particularly in the manufacturing sector where gender segregation is especially strong. But even in mixed-sex groups and service-sector or professional jobs, evidence indicates that patterns of interaction between workers tend to promote the ideas of the suitability of each sex for particular jobs. Joking relationships, flirtations and sexual involvements, and of course sexual harassment, all serve to accentuate the differentiated experience of gender and the idea that "boys will be boys and girls will be girls." For example, Pringle's work on the boss/secretary relationship (1988) shows how the common practices of gossip and "bitching" among female office staff promote the idea that women are unsuited for positions of authority; while work on women in male-dominated professions suggests that women have to choose between compromising their femininity by participating in masculinized social rituals or losing credibility as a colleague by staying aloof (Spencer & Podmore, 1987).

Nonetheless, I have argued elsewhere (Bradley, 1989) that it is easier for women to push into men's jobs than men into women's. Compromised femininity is still a possible female identity; women can take to power dressing, drink and swear with the boys, and wear jeans if need be. The threat to masculinity in entering a women's area is much greater because of the greater visibility and stigmatization of male homosexuality. Indeed there are a number of jobs in which men have long been established, but which still hold such a feminine image that men entering them may automatically be stereotyped as homosexual (hairdressing and dancing, for example). Donnison tells us that men who entered midwifery in the 1830s were denounced in a series of populist pamphlets that portrayed the man-midwife "*both* as a homosexual *and* as a full-time lecher" (Donnison, 1988, p. 60). The same derogation has until very recently been aimed at male nurses, seen stereotypically, according to an officer of one of the British nursing unions, as "either a raving gay or a complete Don Juan." The perceived risk to male heterosexual identity may be so great as to stop many men from even contemplating work as a secretary or a machinist in a garment factory.

Breaking the Barriers:
Challenges to Sex-Typing

However, despite the power of the gendering process, the barriers are not impermeable. Since industrialization there have been numerous cases of women entering male jobs, from clerical work to medicine and law to light engineering work. Often this is the result of the capitalist desire to cut labor costs, as discussed above. The history of the hosiery industry, for example, reveals constant attempts by employers to feminize traditional male jobs. Another important factor historically has been the shortage of male labor in certain periods, notably during wars and in their aftermath. The access of Russian women in the Soviet epoch to all sorts of jobs that in the West were dominated by men (the medical profession, agriculture, and heavy engineering, for example) was almost certainly encouraged by the lack of manpower because of heavy losses sustained by the Soviet armed forces in the Second World War. However, it is also extremely important to consider the role played by women themselves in demanding the right to enter jobs reserved for men. Feminist campaigns in both the nineteenth and twentieth centuries have made equal opportunities in employment a key issue, with some notable successes; and individual women, faced with limited opportunities and determined to earn a decent wage or secure a place in an esteemed profession, have been prepared to endure male abuse, family displeasure, sexual harassment, factory inspectors' raids, and other social sanctions to gain their objectives.

I have suggested that the barriers into women's work are relatively more impermeable. Although masculinization has been less studied, historical study suggests it to be a rarer event. The gains for women entering men's jobs are obvious: better pay, more interesting work; expanded opportunities; power and authority. Men have less to gain from entering women's jobs and, indeed, the analysis above has suggested what they have to lose. Taking up a woman's job will probably mean lower pay and less status and poses a distinct threat to an individual's masculine heterosexual image. It is likely then that men will move into women's jobs only in very special circumstances.

Such a move may occur, for example, at times of general social, economic, and political upheaval, for example, the Industrial Revolution. At these times, social rules are called into question, and new gender norms can emerge. Another precipitating factor is technological change. The invention of a new machine or technique provides a rationale for men to redefine an old female occupation as a man's occupation, thereby increasing its social standing and driving women out or to the margins. Historically, men have used the idea of female technical incompetence to legitimate such moves. Finally, in periods of recession, such as that experienced in Britain in the late 1980s and 1990s, unemployment and lack of opportunities may drive men to consider taking up jobs previously despised as female jobs. Younger men, in particular, whose ideas about work have not been framed by long experience in male work environments, may feel that the prospect of employment is a compensation for any stigma.

Such moves into women's occupations are not necessarily met passively by women. Witz, in her recent study of the medical professions, points to the contestation that surrounds the gendering of occupations. She develops a typology of strategic actions and responses drawing on the Weberian concept of social closure (see also Kreckel, 1980). Dominant groups (usually men) use strategies of exclusion and demarcation against subordinate groups. The idea of *demarcation* refers to a process of internal segregation, whereby the subordinate group is pushed into inferior subspecialties or confined to lower grades. Against these the excluded group can respond with strategies of inclusion (such as the campaigns waged by nineteenth-century women to enter the medical profession) or *dual closure*. The latter refers to the barriers that the subordinate group erects around its own subspecialties to ensure that these, too, are not taken over. Witz shows how the struggles over nurse and midwifery education and registration in the nineteenth and early twentieth centuries involved the use of demarcatory and dual closure strategies (Witz, 1992).

We can see how these various precipitating factors come into play, and the contentious struggles surrounding them, if we consider some examples of how men in the past have entered women's jobs, which I want to relate to three characteristic patterns of entry.

Crossing Over:
Male Entry Into Women's Jobs

In studying women's position in a male-dominated occupational environment, Kanter (1977) pointed to a situation she referred to as *tokenism*, whereby a small number of people of a previously excluded gender are allowed entry into an occupation but remain in a minority. Kanter defined this situation quantitatively; less than 15% was indicative of a token presence. Morgan (1992) has used this term in his recent account of male entry into women's jobs, contrasting it with a situation of "invasion" when the previously excluded gender becomes the dominant one. However, he notes that these processes should not simply be distinguished numerically but relationally: "Women do not have to constitute a statistical majority to constitute an 'invasion.' In terms of masculine perceptions, 'tokens' may signify an invasion" (Morgan, 1992, p. 124). Moreover, Morgan points to the way one situation can shade into another: "the 'tokens' of one decade may be the 'invasion' of the next" (p. 131).

In distinction from Morgan's approach I want to distinguish three rather than two patterns of entry: takeover, invasion, and infiltration.

Takeover. Here a job that was originally assigned to women becomes redesignated as a male specialty, and women are more or less excluded from it.

Invasion. In this case, men move into the occupation in large numbers, although not driving women out completely. Usually, this process is accompanied by processes of internal demarcation and dual closure, whereby men monopolize certain specialties and women monopolize others within the profession or occupation. Usually, though not inevitably, men take the positions at the top of the hierarchy or the higher-status specialties.

Infiltration. This is where a few individual men enter a women's occupation, sometimes for reasons of personal inclination, sometimes because of lack of other employment opportunities. Men may remain as a tiny minority within a female occupation and may have to cope with consequent derogation of their masculinity. Alternatively, if sufficient numbers are drawn into the occupation, the stage is set for invasion or even takeover.

The difference here is not just one of numbers. Each of these patterns also differs in terms of the specific relation between the sexes that develops. In takeover, the task is redefined as a man's job, and women are either excluded or marginalized. Where invasion takes place, the occupation will be less emphatically sex-typed; both women and men will continue working within it, although men will probably maneuver themselves into the powerful positions within it and capture certain specialties through internal demarcation. Finally, where men infiltrate, the occupation will probably remain defined as largely a female one; but men will often exploit their masculine attributes to maximize their career chances within it, while working alongside women.

To illuminate these points further, I will now consider each mode of entry in more detail, weighing the precipitating factors and giving examples in each case.

Takeover

Although, as emphasized in the previous section, it is not uncommon for women to take over male jobs, complete takeover by men of a female occupation is rare, because occupations assigned to women are usually of low social standing and are almost invariably ill-paid. There is little to attract men into them. Moreover, the connotations of femininity surrounding female occupations are, as I argued above, a strong deterrent to men whose masculinity may be jeopardized if they are associated with female work. For men to desire to take over "women's work," then, there seem to be two essential prerequisites. First, men must perceive that there are real economic opportunities offered by the occupation; second, there must be some process of social or technological change occurring, which men can exploit and use to overturn the female associations of the occupation. This may involve a change of name, and in fact this is a persistent feature in all three forms of male entry.

Male takeovers are then most likely to occur at times of major economic upheaval, such as industrialization or the current putative move to a postindustrial service-based economy. Alice Clark cites baking and brewing as two female specialties that were lost to men as a result of the Industrial Revolution in Britain. Commercial expansion, new products and the development of new technologies combined to make baking and brewing attractive economic propositions and to break their association with the home and domesticity; in modernized baking and brewing industries, women have only assistant roles.

As suggested earlier, a technological innovation is often the key to male takeover. Dairy work is another example; Blom shows how, in

Norway in the first half of the twentieth century, milk production became a more important element in the farm economy and therefore ripe for male takeover. However, men were deterred by the traditional female image of the dairy worker, and it was not until milking machines and parlors were introduced that men took hold of this profitable specialty (Blom, 1990). A similar slow takeover occurred in Britain.

Perhaps the classic example of male takeover, however, is cotton spinning. Lazonick's well-known paper (1979) describes the dramatic reversal of roles that occurred with the mechanization of cotton textile production. Whereas in the hand-based cottage industry, women had for centuries specialized in spinning and men had dominated in weaving, the new machines brought new gender allocations, with men operating the spinning mules and women tending the more automated, less complex weaving machines. Walby (1986) argues that even before the move of the industry into the factory, men realized the advantage of capturing the new skill of spinning, because of the heightened productivity (thus increased economic rewards) and because it involved the direction of others' labor. Whereas before the spinner (female) had been seen as doing the preliminary work that enabled the weaver (male) to produce the final product, spinning was to become the key task in mechanized production, with spinners acting as overseers of the factory work team and becoming part of the "aristocracy of labour" (Foster, 1974). Walby argues: "The men utilised their position of power and authority within the household to take control of this new form of profitable employment and direct the labour of the other members of the household, rather than being either a non-participant or directed by the wife" (Walby, 1986, p. 133).

Invasion

These same two factors, technological change and the perception by men of economic opportunities, operated in one of the most notable cases of invasion, the rise of male midwives. Invasion is more common than takeover and tends to involve a more lengthy process of redefinition of the task. It may lead finally to takeover, as was the case with midwifery in America, though not in Britain.

The assigning of a job in manufacturing to women has often been linked to technological change and especially to task degradation (Braverman, 1974). Female jobs in manufacturing are frequently low-skilled, monotonous and repetitive, as well as poorly paid. Studies of the manufacturing industry have frequently revealed men's contempt for and rejection of such jobs (see Cockburn, 1985). Men will truly have to be desperate to take them on. Indeed, during the recessions in Britain in the 1980s and 1990s, it has been reported that men would prefer unemployment to taking such jobs. However, in the service sector, the picture is different. Jobs are less routinized and more flexible, and there is more room for redefinition of both the task itself and its status. Service work, therefore, has witnessed a number of cases of invasion, including mid-wifery. Examples are primary teaching, personnel management, and social work. In these cases, men tend to enter into the profession anticipating that they will be able to make quite rapid career moves into the top posts (primary teaching). Alternatively, the whole profession changes in nature and becomes upgraded (social work and personnel work).

The midwifery case illustrates both the key part that technology can play and the operation of strategies of demarcation. Midwifery had been a traditional female profession in medieval and early modern Europe and was an area where women could both make a good living and earn social and community respect. The financial rewards presumably made it alluring to men, and men-midwives made their appearance in the early seventeenth century; they tended to specialize in births where there were complications and medical intervention was required. But their advance in the profession accelerated rapidly with the invention of the forceps in the early eighteenth century. Thereafter men-midwives, now renamed *accoucheurs*, in line with the leanings of the wealthy and fashionable women who were their initial clients, oversaw the growing medicalization of childbirth; and the traditional female midwives, who did not use forceps, were in danger of being squeezed out altogether. The profession was saved for women partly as a result of the campaigns of various feminist-inspired groups from the 1860s, who struggled to get training and registration for female midwives. Donnison also suggests that the male obstetricians allowed female midwives to continue because they themselves were not interested in attending poorer women from whom only a small charge could be exacted. Tight control of the medical profession in Britain meant, anyway, that the supply of doctors was limited. In America, where regulation was looser and competition for patients greater, the profession of midwife was crushed out altogether as childbirth came totally under the medical control of doctors. In the early twentieth century many states made midwifery illegal (Donnison, 1988).

In the case of midwifery, male and female interests came rather starkly into conflict. Such clashes are often solved by parceling out different specialties between men and women, sometimes openly by strategies of dual closure, sometimes more informally. The case of men in nursing illustrates this, and will be discussed under the heading of infiltration.

British personnel work, as described by Legge (1987), provides another example of a slow process of invasion, involving redefinition of an occupation. In what was originally known as "welfare work," women were the pioneers. This arose from the involvement of Victorian upper- and middle-class women in all types of philanthropic and charitable work, what Matthaei (1982) has described in the American case as "social homemaking." While the domestic ideology frowned upon women in paid employment, social homemaking was seen as a suitable activity for which women's superior moral qualities fitted them. From this tradition arose the contemporary social work profession and welfare work in factories. This commenced in the early twentieth century and was encouraged by the recruitment of women into munitions work during the war. Because the employment of women in factory work was officially discouraged, female factory workers, unlike men, were considered in need of protection and advice, which middle-class women could provide. In 1927 the Institute of Industrial Welfare (which was to become the Institute of Personnel Management in 1931) had 420 members, of whom only 20 were men (Legge, 1987).

The sex of personnel workers changed as the job expanded to include dealing with labor relations more generally, including recruitment, and especially with the management of industrial relations. Women were not seen as tough enough or having the relevant experience for these latter specialties, though they might continue to work as "lady assistants," dealing specifically with the personal welfare problems of female staff. The change in name, from industrial welfare to personnel management, was a signal of the masculinization of the occupation—management being, of course, a generally masculine function. The invasion by men gathered momentum in the post-1945 period, when industrial relations was a high-profile area; by 1970, 80% of IPM members were male (Legge, 1987). Men, thus, while not entirely driving out women from what was still seen as the most suitable aspect of management for them, had succeeded in redefining the functions of the profession, raising its status and capturing the highest grade posts for themselves—a classic case of invasion.

Infiltration

Of the three routes, infiltration is the hardest to trace, to quantify, and to analyze. Individual and "pioneer" men may choose to take up women's work for all sorts of personal reasons, such as interests, talents, or inclinations; distaste for stereotypically macho environments; or desire to work jointly with a partner or to remain within a particular neighborhood. Considerable numbers of men have been drawn to nontraditional masculine activities, such as needlework or the care of young children. If sufficient numbers of men enter an area (like primary school teaching), then the process of invasion may be under way. But, as individuals, many men have no particular interest in either changing the content or status of a job or driving women out. Such men may be happy simply to work within a predominantly female environment.

It is important to note that in most societies there is no single definition of masculinity or masculine activity. Although in most Western societies the dominant or hegemonic form of masculinity (Brittan, 1989; Connell, 1987) may be traditional heterosexual masculinity of the more macho variety, alternatives evolve. Many men may reject hegemonic masculinity and aspire to other forms of masculine identity, such as that of the "new man," the male feminist, or the various forms of homosexual male identity. Although we so far have little account of why individual men choose to enter women's work, the adoption of such identities may be a contributory factor.

Ethnic communities also offer different versions of masculine behavior. Migration, therefore, may have an important role in challenging sex-typing. For example, cigar-making changed its gender ascription from female to male and back to female in America because of the employment of first male, then female migrants from central and Eastern Europe where the work was traditionally done by girls and women (Wertheimer, 1977). White British males have not traditionally been employed as sewing machine operators (although they have worked in the garment industry as skilled cutters and tailors) and are said by employers to reject such feminine work. But Asian males may have no such cultural inhibitions and bring with them skills and experience gained in cultures where operating such machines is not sex-typed as an exclusively feminine activity. Asian men have been employed, for example, as machine operators in the Leicester hosiery industry.

Another reason for male infiltration may be lack of opportunity, especially in a period of high unemployment. Young men or older men who have become unemployed may find it impossible to procure men's work in their locality. There is some evidence that in the recent recessionary periods in Britain men have started taking up "female" jobs like cashiering in supermarkets, word-processing, or secretarial work. Because this may be a matter of compulsion rather than choice, it is possible that this may lead in the future to some degree of redefinition of tasks, or to men operating strategies of demarcation (young men, for example, may operate tills as part of a general process of learning retailing skills, while women are simply confined to the single task). Pringle's study of Australian secretaries (1988) suggests that because of the ridicule commonly expressed at the idea of men working in the occupation, male secretaries frequently negotiate alternative job titles, such as "personal assistant" or "information officer," or even "trouble shooter." This process of renaming, which we have seen to be a common event, illustrates the power of discourses of gender and the difficulty involved in moving beyond them. Pringle's study indicates that this is not just a problem of men refusing to relinquish masculine superiority. Women cling as strongly to stereotyped ideas, reacting adversely to the concepts of male secretaries and female bosses.

Male nurses in Britain have similarly had to struggle against stereotypes, particularly in the twentieth century when nursing has become established in people's minds as a female job. Nursing sits on the boundary between infiltration and invasion, but I classify it as the former because it still retains its female image. In fact, the numbers of men in nursing have fluctuated over time. Dingwall, Rafferty, and Webster (1988) point to the presence of men working as nurses from the beginning of the nineteenth century, although women dominated in what had been a longstanding female occupation. Men resorted to internal demarcation to construct a role for themselves in the profession. While women predominated as general caregivers for the sick, men took a more specialized role as medical attendants in hospitals. They acted as assistants and subordinates of physicians and apothecaries; their role was to apply the technical treatments of "heroic medicine"—all the blisterings, bleedings, and purgings—and to attend to dressings and wounds. Another area in which men predominated was asylum nursing, which was thought inappropriate for women as it involved dealing with violent patients, sometimes confronting obscenity and abuse, and required considerable physical strength. Also, Dingwall et al. point out that in the rural settings where asylums were normally located, basic agricultural and handyman skills were often required of attendants.

When nursing was reformed by Nightingale and others, the women who ran the profession worked hard to keep men out of other areas of nursing. The Royal College of Nursing did not admit men until the postwar period, and chances of advancement for men were limited by the 1919 Nurses Act (Bellaby & Oribabor, 1980; Carpenter, 1977). But Carpenter argues that the reforms of the National Health Service, which started in the 1960s and have proceeded along managerial principles, opened up the way for men to get into higher positions in the nursing hierarchy; they were seen to possess managerial aptitudes considered lacking in women. Although men are still a minority in general nursing, their numbers are increasing and they are disproportionately represented in higher grades.

In her discussion of groups who are numerically in a minority, Kanter (1977) stresses the disadvantages experienced by token women because of their visibility: They are perpetually on show, their performance being appraised; they are subject to stereotyping processes, whereby their individual characteristics are distorted to fit the general views about women; and their differences from the majority are exaggerated because of their prominence. Kanter argues that this applies to all minorities, including male ones. But this overlooks the positive cultural valuation given to male attributes in our society. Thus, the visibility of male nurses has, in Britain anyway, become an advantage rather than a handicap. By virtue of their maleness, male nurses are seen as more career-oriented, ambitious, and fit for managerial roles, and consequently ascend career ladders more rapidly than female colleagues. Thus, in Britain, infiltration moves toward invasion.

Infiltration, invasion, and takeover may be conceptualized as three stages on a continuum of the masculinization of an occupation. However, although there may be a progression through all three stages, it is not necessarily the case. Infiltration of men in nursing has not yet proceeded to wholesale invasion, and it might not be in the interests of existing male nurses for this to happen; at present they occupy a disproportionate number of top posts within the profession. Some men may prefer to work in a more feminine environment. By contrast, takeover and invasion may occur without a lengthy period of infiltration, as in the case of cotton-spinning outlined above. Moreover, as I have indicated, there are different relational outcomes in each case, especially in terms of the sex-typing of a job. There are also differences in the characteristic precipitating factors in each case. Takeover is particularly associated with major social and technological changes; invasion relates to a more evolutionary process of redefinition of tasks; while infiltration is linked to individual motivation and to recession and lack of openings for men in traditional male jobs.

Conclusion

This essay has indicated the blocks to men's crossing over and has highlighted the circumstances in which they may wish to do so. Three aspects appear especially crucial. Two of these relate to the factors that may either attract men into crossing over or deter them from doing so. The first is the absence or presence of the lure of economic rewards, either in terms of promising career prospects or in lack of alternative opportunities. The second key issue is the problem of damaged masculinity, which may result from entering a woman's job, and the development of new masculinities that may encourage men to overturn stereotypes. I am thus laying stress on the active role of men themselves in making choices and changing the patterns of segregation. However, the third crucial factor is an external one: technological change, which often produces the context for the de-gendering or re-gendering of tasks. Technological change is not an absolutely necessary condition for crossing over (witness the case of personnel work), but continues to be an important influence on current renegotiation of the gender order in employment.

Male crossover is likely to remain low while women's jobs continue to be ill paid. Although recession may have the effect of pushing men to look beyond traditional male options, it also encourages employers to cut costs further in order to be more competitive, leading to further downwards pressure on women's wage rates. The achievement of equal pay and the revaluation of women's skills thus seem necessary preconditions for any real breakdown of the segregation barrier. It is also necessary that discourses and ideologies of masculinity and femininity become further weakened and fragmented, to allow people to move freely between activities without feeling their personal identity and status diminished or impaired. Unless these changes occur, men will probably cling to their existing advantages and seek to stay in traditionally male jobs, or to erect internal boundaries within feminine jobs they invade in order to maintain their expected male edge.

Feminism, on both counts, has a crucial role to play in breaking down structures of sex-typing. Men themselves will also need to change, in working to rid themselves of expectations of superiority to women in terms of status, authority, and rewards, and in contributing to a revaluation of caring and interpersonal skills and the challenge to the hegemonic versions of masculinity.

References

Baker, E. (1964). *Technology and women's work.* New York: Columbia University Press.

Bellaby, P., & Oribabor, P. (1980). The history of the present—Contradiction and struggle in nursing. In C. Davies (Ed.), *Rewriting nursing history* (pp. 147-174). London: Croom Helm.

Blom, I. (1990). Changing gender identities in an industrializing society: The case of Norway. *Gender and History, 2*(2), 131-147.

Boserup, E. (1970). *Women's role in economic development.* New York: St. Martin's Press.

Bradley, H. (1989). *Men's work, women's work.* Cambridge: Polity Press.

Braverman, H. (1974). *Labor and monopoly capital.* New York: Monthly Review Press.

Brittan, A. (1989). *Masculinity and power.* Oxford: Basil Blackwell.

Carpenter, M. (1977). The new managerialism and professionalism in nursing. In M. Stacey, M. Reid, C. Heath, & R. Dingwall (Eds.), *Health and the division of labour.* London: Croom Helm.

Clark, A. (1982). *Working life of women in the seventeenth century.* London: Routledge.

Cockburn, C. (1983). *Brothers.* London: Pluto.

Cockburn, C. (1985). *Machinery of dominance.* London: Pluto.

Cockburn, C. (1991). *In the way of women.* London: Macmillan.

Connell, R. (1987). *Gender and power.* Cambridge: Polity Press.

Dingwall, R., Rafferty, A. M., & Webster, C. (1988). *An introduction to the social history of nursing.* London: Routledge.

Donnison, J. (1988). *Midwives and medical men.* London: Historical Publications.

Foster, J. (1974). *Class struggle and the industrial revolution.* London: Weidenfeld.

Hakim, C. (1979). *Occupational segregation by sex* (Department of Employment Research Paper No. 9). London: HMSO.

Hall, C. (1979). The early formation of Victorian domestic ideology. In S. Burman (Ed.), *Fit work for women* (pp. 15-32). London: Croom Helm.

Hartmann, H. (1976). Patriarchy, capitalism and job segregation by sex. *Signs, 1*(3), 137-168.

Holcombe, L. (1973). *Victorian ladies at work.* Newton Abbott, UK: David and Charles.

Jenson, J., Hagen, E., & Reddy, C. (1988). *The feminization of the labour force.* Cambridge: Polity Press.

Kanter, R. M. (1977). *Men and women of the corporation.* New York: Basic Books.

Kreckel, R. (1980). Unequal opportunities structure and labour market segmentation. *Sociology, 14,* 525-550.

Lazonick, W. (1979). Industrial relations and technical change: The case of the self-acting mule. *Cambridge Journal of Economics, 1*(4), 231-262.

Legge, K. (1987). Women in personnel management: Uphill climb or downward slide. In A. Spencer, & D. Podmore, *In a man's world* (pp. 33-60). London: Tavistock.

Lown, J. (1990). *Women and industrialization.* Cambridge: Polity Press.

Mallier, A., & Rosser, M. (1987). *Women and the economy.* London: Macmillan.

Matthaei, J. (1982). *An economic history of women in America.* Brighton: Harvester.

Morgan, D. (1992). *Discovering men*. London: Routledge.

Oakley, A. (1976). *Housewife*. Harmondsworth, UK: Penguin.

Ortner, S. (1974). Is female to male as nature is to culture? In M. Rosaldo & L. Lamphere (Eds.), *Women, culture and society* (pp. 67-87). Palo Alto, CA: Stanford University Press.

Pringle, R. (1988). *Secretaries talk*. London: Verso.

Reskin, B. F., & Roos, P. A. (1990). *Job queues, gender queues: Explaining women's inroads into occupation*. Philadelphia: Temple University Press.

Spencer, A., & Podmore, D. (1987). *In a man's world: Essays on women in male-dominated professions*. London: Tavistock.

Walby, S. (1986). *Patriarchy at work*. Cambridge: Polity Press.

Wertheimer, B. (1977). *We were there*. New York: Pantheon.

Witz, A. (1992). *Professions and patriarchy*. London: Routledge.

Zimmeck, M. (1986). Jobs for girls: The expansion of clerical work for women, 1850-1914. In A. John (Ed.), *Unequal opportunities* (pp. 153-177). Oxford: Basil Blackwell.

3

The Pay of Men in "Female" Occupations

Is Comparable Worth Only for Women?

PAULA ENGLAND
MELISSA S. HERBERT

In the paid workplace, the two most familiar types of sex discrimination against women are (a) discrimination in hiring or placement and (b) lack of equal pay for equal work in the same job. In the United States, these traditionally recognized types of discrimination are violations of Title VII of the Civil Rights Act. In contrast, the courts have not interpreted this or other federal laws to prohibit the sort of discrimination at issue in comparable worth (England, 1992, Chapter 5). Comparable worth refers to a distinct third type of sex discrimination. Here, the sex composition of jobs affects their wage level, so that jobs filled largely by men pay more than comparable jobs filled largely by women. "Comparability" is assessed by a job evaluation that gives points for various job demands, so that jobs receiving the same number of points are considered comparable although they may involve distinct tasks. Employers may assign lower pay levels to jobs filled largely by women because they underestimate the contribution to organizations' bottom line goals of the work done in "female" occupations, or because they see women as "needing" or "deserving" lower earnings than men. Even absent such motivations, if these factors dictated lower wages in female jobs in the past, institutional inertia will maintain lower relative wages for women's jobs for decades.

The sort of wage discrimination at issue in comparable worth disadvantages women relative to men, on average, since more women than men are in predominantly female occupations. Thus, the sex gap in pay would be smaller if this sort of discrimination did not exist. However, given the focus of this volume on men in "female" jobs, it is of interest whether these men are victims of the wage discrimination at issue in comparable worth, even though it advantages most men (those in "male" jobs). To explore this, we review past research showing that men in predominantly female occupations earn less than men in comparable male jobs. We then explore how to theorize about the sort of wage discrimination at issue in comparable worth. Finally, we present an analysis, using 1980 Census data, showing that men, as well as women, earn less if employed in a predominantly female occupation than if employed in a comparable occupation containing more males.

Past Empirical Research

A large body of research has shown that a job's sex composition affects the wage rate that is offered to either men or women in the job. One type of study has taken U.S. Census detailed occupational categories as units of analysis and used national data. Such studies have controlled for occupational characteristics such as average requirements for education, and an array of occupational demands, with measures typically taken from the *Dictionary of Occupational Titles* (U.S. Department of Labor, 1977). Such studies have found that, controlling for occupations' demands, both men and women earn less if they work in a predominantly female occupation. This has been found for 1940, 1950, 1960 (Treiman & Terrell, 1975), and 1970 (Ferber & Lowry, 1976) with controls for education (Treiman & Terrell, 1975); for 1970 with controls for education, skill measures from the *Dictionary of Occupational Titles*, and other variables (England, Chassie, & McCormick, 1982; England & McLaughlin, 1979); and for 1980 with even more elaborate controls (Aldrich & Buchele, 1986; England, 1992; Parcel, 1989). Only one study failed to find this negative effect of occupational percent female (Filer, 1989). England (1992, Chapter 3) argues that Filer included inappropriate variables and thus "overpartialed" the effect.

A second type of study takes individuals as units of analysis, and examines the effects of occupational sex composition by mapping this contextual variable onto each individual's record, according to the occupation he or she holds. Controls for various other occupational characteristics are mapped on in the same way, as contextual variables. In such studies, separate regressions are run for men and women, and individuals' human capital (education and actual or estimated experience) is controlled. These studies also find a net negative effect on both men's and women's wages of being in an occupation that is predominantly female (Johnson & Solon, 1986; O'Neill, 1983; Sorensen, 1984). One study (England, Farkas, Kilbourne, & Dou, 1988) found this negative effect of occupational percent female, using longitudinal data and a "fixed-effects" model to control for any unmeasured differences between unchanging pay-relevant attributes of those individuals selected into predominantly female and male occupations. That is, the study found that when individuals change occupations, their earnings tend to go down if they move to an occupation containing a higher percentage of females than their previous occupation, and to go up if they move to an occupation with a higher percentage of men. These effects held after adjusting for any changes in the individuals' human capital, and for demands of the occupations as measured by the *Dictionary of Occupational Titles*.

All of these studies have examined the effect of occupational sex composition on male and female earnings separately. (The exception is Treiman and Terrell, 1975, which looked at effects on male earnings only.) All found that the negative effect of the percent female of one's occupation on wages held for men as well as women. Thus, net of the controls, women in female occupations earn less than women in male occupations, and men in female occupations earn less than men in male occupations.[1] Sorensen (1989) has assembled many of these studies and used their results to make some computations. She calculated that the magnitude of the effect of occupational sex composition on wages is such that this wage discrimination explains between 10% and 30% (depending on the study) of the overall sex gap in pay among full-time workers.[2]

A third type of study uses data from one organization or employer. One advantage of these studies is that they often employ more detailed job categories than do national studies. A second advantage is that they allow us to see the potential effects of comparable worth at the level they occur in the version of the reform generally advocated— within a single employer or organization. A disadvantage of such studies is that they are limited to the public sector where data on pay are more readily available. A number of states have done job evaluation studies for comparable worth purposes in the past 10 years. These studies show that, net of measures of job skill or worth, female jobs pay less (Acker, 1989; Baron & Newman, in press; Orazem & Mattila, 1989; Remick, 1984; Rothchild, 1984; Steinberg, Haignere, Possin, Chertos, & Treiman, 1986). For our purposes, a drawback of these studies is that they generally do not provide a separate analysis for men and women, but rather used the bottom, top, or midpoint of the policy-set wage band for each job as the dependent variable. Thus, while a fairly safe presumption is that *both* men and women in female jobs are suffering from comparable worth discrimination when such discrimination is detected, the published analyses do not specifically document that men as well as women in female jobs suffer a wage penalty.

Other studies have analyzed how change over time in jobs' sex composition affects change in their pay, finding that when a job changes its sex composition, the wage for both men and women goes up if more males come into the job, and the wage for both men and women goes down if more women come into the job (Ferber & Lowry, 1976, p. 384; Pfeffer & Davis-Blake, 1987). We cannot be sure whether these studies indicate that the changing sex composition affected the wages, as these authors suggest, or whether the change in wage affects sex composition such that men resist women's entrance into "their" occupations less when wages are declining relative to other fields, as suggested by Reskin and Roos (1990), or whether both effects are operative.

Overall, past studies find ample evidence that men as well as women are penalized by being employed in a predominantly female occupation. How has such wage discrimination been theorized?

Theorizing Comparable Worth

The various mechanisms through which women are subordinated to men can be usefully summarized in two distinct categories: (a) discouraging women's entry into highly rewarded positions seen as male and (b) devaluation and allocation of low rewards for positions seen as female. These two categories differ in the mechanism of subordination they thematize, but they are not mutually exclusive. We believe that both operate simultaneously.

How do these two mechanisms affect men? Overall, both mechanisms work to the advantage of men relative to women. However, the second mechanism can be a source of subordination for those men who, for whatever reason, find themselves in a traditionally female role. Since it is the second mechanism that is at issue in comparable worth, our theoretical discussion focuses on how various feminist and sociological theories understand this process of devaluation and underreward to operate.

Normative portions of feminist theories argue that sexism *should* not be allowed to continue, while positive portions explain mechanisms of women's subordination to men. Most sociological theories confine themselves to positive claims; thus sociological and feminist theories overlap in their explanation of sexism.

How is the devaluation of positions because they are associated with women theorized by feminist and sociological theories? Problematizing the devaluation of female roles has not been a major theme of liberal feminist theory; rather, its emphasis has been on the exclusion of women from traditionally male public roles. Nonetheless, organizations generally labeled liberal feminist, such as the National Organization for Women and National Women's Political Caucus, have advocated comparable worth, seeing it as an issue of equity or equal treatment to require that employers use consistent standards to evaluate and pay male and female occupations (England, 1992, Chapter 6). However, liberal feminists have not emphasized the common mechanism behind devaluing the work women do in the private sphere of the home and the work women do in paid employment.

Feminists working within a Marxist tradition have, more than liberal feminists, recognized a common logic behind the devaluation of women's household work and female occupations in paid employment. In the case of household work, the Marxist-feminist position articulated in the "domestic labor debates" is that the work of homemakers, through producing labor power (of the current and next generation of wage workers), contributes to capitalist profit and thereby involves exploitation (James & Dalla Costa, 1973; Shelton & Agger, 1993; Vogel, 1983). Marxists see sex discrimination in employment, whether it involves keeping women out of male jobs or devaluing female jobs, as a divide-and-conquer strategy that serves to strengthen capitalists vis-à-vis workers. Thus, while Marxists have been more likely than liberal feminists to see a common logic underlying the devaluation of work labeled "female" in the household and in paid labor, for them the common logic is capitalism rather than sexism. We, along with socialist-feminists (e.g., Hartmann, 1976), dissent from this view and argue that it is a mistake to reduce sexism to an epiphenomenon of capitalism.

The feminist theorizing that most emphasizes the devaluation of all roles associated with women is sometimes referred to as cultural feminism,[3] which we see as a subset of radical feminism. Radical feminists see women's subordination to be *the* fundamental inequality, not the side effect of class inequalities that orthodox Marxists and Marxist-feminists see it to be. Some radical feminists see the deprecation of women as one part of an ancient historical move from cooperative, egalitarian societies to patriarchy, which introduced a hierarchical ("power-over") model of the relationship between gods and men, men and women, and humans and nature (Eisler, 1987; Starhawk, 1987; Tuana, in press). Some radical feminists believe that women's subordination is primarily the result of how sexuality, childbearing, and child rearing have been socially organized (Jaggar, 1983). Because activities in these spheres have been seen as female and deprecated, there is a clear link to cultural feminism.

Cultural feminists value traditionally female characteristics, disputing the traditional deprecation of qualities viewed as feminine (Alcoff, 1988; Donovan, 1985, Chapter 2). Thus, whereas patriarchal and liberal views have elevated the spiritual or rational over the physical, emotional, or intuitive, cultural feminists argue for at least an equal valuation of the latter qualities. Where patriarchal views revere the bravery of risking one's life in hunting, sport, or war, the cultural feminist reveres nurturing for its preservation of life at least equally. Whereas patriarchal thinkers, classical liberals, and some Marxists have revered humans for their domination over nature, cultural feminism reveres harmony with nature. Cultural feminists argue that people have always benefitted from the work performed by women, but patriarchal cultures do not acknowledge this contribution to the extent that the value of male positions is acknowledged. Rather, the characteristics one needs to do female nurturant work have been seen as weakness, lack of proper individuation, or lack of rationality, and the work itself has been devalued.

Work that we would classify as cultural feminist includes critiques by scholars in several disciplines of the way that nurturant work and emotional connections have been devalued by Western culture because of their association with women. For example, feminists have protested the way in which the contributions to human development made by the emotional nurturance provided by mothers and other caretakers (usually female) have been downplayed by developmental and clinical psychologists (Chodorow, 1978; Gilligan, 1982; C. Keller, 1986; Kittay &

Meyers, 1987). Another example of the devaluation of emotions is the tendency of philosophers of science to regard emotional connection as a contaminating distorter rather than a possible route to knowledge (E. F. Keller, 1985; Schott, 1988). The disinclination to use words denoting "work" for nurturant work in earlier sociological theories is also evidence of such devaluation. This can be seen in the words Parsons (1954) chose for his famous instrumental/expressive distinction. He chose the term *expressive* to describe the role of child rearing and homemaking, a term that connotes self-indulgence rather than work.

Where sociological theories could more usefully join cultural feminist theory is in elucidating the mechanisms by which greater rewards for roles seen as male are perpetuated. We make some very general suggestions, but see this as largely uncharted terrain because sociologists and cultural/radical feminists have each paid little attention to the writings of the other. Sociological notions of institutional inertia help explain the perpetuation of low rewards for female jobs in formal organizations, as these arrangements are embedded in wage systems, and organizations then seldom reconsider the relative rankings of jobs. Some of the value produced in female roles, particularly when it involves nurturance and emotion, is negated by the many linguistic conventions that deprecate emotion. Organized strategic action by men to procure higher rewards for male-typical work is also relevant. In sum, we suggest that the relevant social mechanisms involved in the devaluation of "female" roles include institutions, encoded cultural values, and purposive collective action.

Data and Methods for the Empirical Analysis

The analysis will ascertain whether men who are employed in occupations in which a higher percentage of workers are women earn less than men employed in comparable occupations containing more males. For comparison, we present analogous results for women. A necessary part of operationalizing this question is determining what we mean by "comparable" jobs. We will use an approach similar to that used in policy-capturing job evaluations used in pay equity studies within a single employer. (On methods of job evaluation, see England, 1992, Chapter 4; Steinberg & Haignere, 1987.) Such studies give each job points on each of a number of compensable criteria. We use variables available on national occupational data that are similar to measures generally measured in job evaluations in one organization: measures of requirements for cognitive skill and education, responsibility for other workers, and onerous physical working conditions. Since we are using national data rather than data from a single organization, some inter-occupational pay differences in these data come from the differential placement of occupations across marginal industries and firms. Comparable worth as a reform is generally not envisioned to deal with between-employer pay differences generated by industrial and firm characteristics. Thus, we control for industrial and organizational variables that could otherwise distort our estimates of the tendency to offer lower wages to female occupations than to comparable male occupations.

The analysis uses a dataset in which 1980 Census detailed (3-digit) occupations are the units of analysis. All jobs have been categorized by the Census Bureau into 503 occupational categories. All data presented in this chapter are based on the 403 occupations that do not have missing values on any of the variables used in this analysis.[4]

The analysis uses ordinary-least-squares multiple regression. Separate regressions are run for men and women. The male and female analyses have the same 403 occupations as their units of analysis, but differ in their dependent variable and weights, as explained below. We will present one-tailed tests of statistical significance, since we predict positive effects on earnings of each of the three independent variables chosen to reflect compensable criteria common to job evaluations, and we predict a negative effect of occupations' percent female.

Our variables, along with data sources for each, are listed in Table 3.1. We identify each variable with a short, descriptive name, given in capital letters, and describe each below. Table 3.2 contains the results of the regression analyses. Many variables were converted to standardized (Z) scores prior to computing the regression, as indicated by the Z in their variable names.[5] Variables not converted to standardized scores are expressed in percentage points (% FEMALE, % UNION, % HAZARDS, % GOVT, % SELF-EMPLOYED), as a 0-1 dummy variable (AUTHORITY), in numbers of people (NUMBER MEN, FTYR, and NUMBER WOMEN, FTYR) or in dollars (MMEANHR and FMEANHR).

Average Male and Female Earnings. The two dependent variables are average male hourly earnings (MMEANHR) and average female hourly earnings (FMEANHR) of full-time year-round workers in the occupation in 1980. MMEANHR is the dependent variable in the male regression; FMEANHR is the dependent variable in the female regression.

Table 3.1 Description of Variables Used in Regression Analysis

Variable	Description	Source[1]	N[2]
SEX COMPOSITION			
% FEMALE	% Female of all FTYR wkrs in occ	U.S. Census 1980	503
COGNITIVE SKILL AND TRAINING DEMANDS			
COMPLEXITY W/DATA	Complexity of task w/data	DOT	495
GEN'L EDUC	General education (schooling)	DOT	495
INTELLIGENCE	Intelligence	DOT	495
NUMERICAL APTITUDE	Numerical aptitude	DOT	495
VERBAL APTITUDE	Verbal aptitude	DOT	495
FEM EDUC	Mean education in years of women in occ	Census-P.U.M.S.	502
MALE EDUC	Mean education in years of men in occ	Census-P.U.M.S.	503
FEM PERCENT COLLEGE	% women have 4 or more years college	Census-P.U.M.S.	502
MALE PERCENT COLLEGE	% men have 4 or more years college	Census-P.U.M.S.	503
VOC OR OJT TRAINING	Vocational or on-the-job training time, in months	DOT	495
LEARN NEW THINGS	Need to learn new things on the job	Filer, QES	432
ZCOGNITIVE FACTOR	Factor created with above 11 variables; principal components factor analysis	Created by Author	430
RESPONSIBILITY FOR OTHER WORKERS			
AUTHORITY	Dummy variable for whether occ involves supr or mgr authority over other wkrs	Coded by Author	503
PHYSICAL WORKING CONDITIONS			
% HAZARDS	% wkrs face physical hazards	DOT	495
INDUSTRIAL AND ORGANIZATIONAL CHARACTERISTICS			
% GOVT	% wkrs in occ work for fed, state, or local government	Census-P.U.M.S.	502
% SELF-EMPLOYED	% in occ who are self-employed	Census-P.U.M.S.	502
% UNION	% of wkrs in occ in a union	Filer, KLK	432

Table 3.1 Continued

Variable	Description	Source[1]	N[2]
ZINDUS CAP INTENS	Occ mn of industries' assets per employee	Hodson	497
ZINDUS OLIGOPOLY	Occ mn of industries' % of sales by top 8 firms	Hodson	473
ZINDUS FOR DIVIDENDS	Occ mn of industries' mn $ of dividends from foreign subsid per firm	Hodson	497
ZINDUS SALES TO GOVT	Occ mn of industries' $ of sales to government per $ tot sales	Hodson	497
ZINDUS SALES PER WKR	Occ mn of industries' $ of sales per employee	Hodson	473
ZINDUS PROFITS	Occ mn of industries' net income per $ value of assets	Hodson	473
ZINDUS SALES PER FIRM	Occ mn of industries' mean sales per firm	Hodson	475
EARNINGS			
FEMALE HOURLY EARNINGS	Mn hourly earnings of women in ECLF who worked FTYR in 1979	U.S. Census 1980	503
MALE HOURLY EARNINGS	Mn hourly earnings of men in ECLF who worked FTYR in 1979	U.S. Census 1980	503
WEIGHTS			
NUMBER WOMEN, FTYR	Number women working in occ FTYR, 1979	U.S. Census 1980	503
NUMBER MEN, FTYR	Number men working in occ FTYR, 1979	U.S. Census 1980	503

SOURCES: [1]Key to Sources (See England, 1992, for further details):
  Census P.U.M.S. = U.S. Census, 1980, Public-Use Micro-Data Sample
  DOT = *Dictionary of Occupational Titles* (4th ed.)
  Filer = Data provided by Randall Filer (1989)
  Hodson = Data on industrial characteristics provided by Hodson (1983)
  KLK = Measure from Kokkelenberg and Sockell (1985)
  QES = Quality of Employment Survey, University of Michigan
  U.S. Census 1980 = Published volumes from 1980 Census
[2]Number of non-missing values for this variable.
Abbreviations used: ECLF = experienced civilian labor force; FTYR = full-time year-round; mgr = manager; mn = mean; occ = occupation; subsid = subsidiaries; supr = supervisor; w/ = with; wkr = worker

Weights. Two variables are used to weight the analyses. These are measures of the number of men (NUMBER MEN, FTYR) and number of women (NUMBER WOMEN, FTYR) among the full-time year-round workers in each occupation. Thus, the female means and regression are weighted such that occupations containing more women "count" more, and analogously for men.

Sex Composition. The independent variable of major interest is the % FEMALE (from 0 to 100) of those who were employed full-time year-round in the occupation in 1980. The occupation with the highest percent female was secretary, of which 98.8% were women. Typists, childcare workers, and dental assistants were also more than 97% female. There were 18 occupations containing more than 99% males in 1980. They include architects, firefighters, auto mechanics, plumbers, and supervisors in a number of blue-collar trades.

Cognitive Skill and Training Demands. The amount of cognitive skill and training required by occupations is a concept for which many detailed measures are available. Because many of them are highly correlated, if all these variables were entered into the same regression, estimates of their separate effects would be hampered by multi-collinearity, a statistical problem produced when independent variables are so highly correlated that attempts to isolate their individual effects produce coefficients that are highly unstable from sample to sample. Our solution to this problem was to combine 11 measures of cognitive skill and training (listed in Table 3.1) into one measure through a factor analysis. The principal component analysis yielded only one factor with an eigenvalue above 1. (For information on factor loadings, see England, 1992.) The regression analysis reported in this chapter used this ZCOGNITIVE FACTOR in place of these variables. Many of the variables making up the ZCOGNITIVE FACTOR are from the *Dictionary of Occupational Titles* (U.S. Department of Labor, 1977).

Responsibility for Other Workers. Most job evaluations give points for supervision or management of other workers, conceptualizing this as a type of responsibility. This was measured with a dummy variable called AUTHORITY, which was coded 1 if the job involved management or supervision of other workers and 0 otherwise. Basically, those coded 1 were all occupations with the word *manager* or *supervisor* in the title. They included lower, middle, and upper levels of management in both the public, private, and not-for-profit sectors, as well as foremen (*sic*) and other supervisors of blue-collar workers. (For a list of all occupations coded 1, see England, 1992.)

Physical Working Conditions. Having to do tasks that involve physical hazards (% HAZARDS) is a characteristic for which many job evaluations give points. Our measure of hazards, taken from the *Dictionary of Occupational Titles* (U.S. Department of Labor, 1977), indicates the percentage of workers in the occupation whose work typically involves any of the following: proximity to moving mechanical parts or electrical shock, working in high places with danger of falling, and exposure to burns, explosives, or toxic agents.

Industrial and Organizational Characteristics. Research on economic segmentation finds that some organizations and some industries pay more than others to workers with equivalent qualifications (Beck, Horan, & Tolbert, 1978; Coverdill, 1988; Farkas, England, & Barton, 1988; Kalleberg, Wallace, & Althauser, 1981). This could affect occupational earnings to the extent that some occupations are concentrated in particular industries or types of organizations. Thus, the regression models used in this analysis include, as controls, measures of the characteristics of the organizations and industries in which incumbents in each occupation are likely to work. The distinction between an occupation and industry is that an occupation defines the function one performs, while an industry is defined by the product (good or service) that firms in the industry sell or provide. Thus the secretary and car assembler working for General Motors are in different occupations but the same industry. Janitors who work for IBM, for a city, and for a store are in the same occupation but different industries.

Earnings may vary by whether one is self-employed, works for government, or works in the private sector. Measures of the percent of an occupation's workers who worked for government (% GOVT) and were self-employed (% SELF-EMPLOYED) were included. To avoid multicollinearity, the percent of workers in private industry was not included because it is highly negatively correlated with the percent working in government. Roughly speaking, coefficients for % GOVT and % SELF-EMPLOYED can be interpreted as the effects of working for government or being self-employed compared to working in the private sector. We also included a measure of the percentage of workers in the occupation who are unionized (% UNION), averaged for a 3-year period centered upon 1980.

Occupational averages for several industrial characteristics that affect wages were also included. Measures originally coded for each industry were converted into occupational averages, according to the likelihood of members of the occupation working in each industry. The final variables are normalized transformations of these occupational averages for measures of the capital intensity (ZINDUS CAP INTENS) of production, measured by the average assets of firms in the industry per employee; ZINDUS OLIGOPOLY, what percent of all sales in the industry go to the top eight firms; ZINDUS FOR DIVIDENDS, average dollar dividends from foreign subsidiaries per firm; ZINDUS SALES TO GOVT, the percent of sales (in dollars) going to the government among firms in the industry; ZINDUS SALES PER WORKER, dollars of sales per employee; ZINDUS PROFITS, net income per dollar value of assets, and ZINDUS SALES PER FIRM, the average dollars of sales per firm. (For details, see England, 1992, Chapter 3.) These industrial measures tell us the tendency of those in an occupation to be in industries with a particular characteristic. Thus, for example, ZINDUS SALES PER WORKER tells us the sales per firm of the industry the "average" person in a given occupation was in, in a metric such that a score of 1 means that the occupation was one standard deviation above or below the score for the average occupation on this variable.

Findings on Determinants of Occupations' Pay

Job Evaluation Variables

Table 3.2 shows the results of the regression analysis. Looking first at effects of variables in a standard job evaluation, we see that both men and women earn more if they are in an occupation that scores high on the factor measuring cognitive skill and training. Since the factor score is in standardized form, the coefficients of 1.235 for women and 1.972 for men indicate that a one standard deviation increase in the factor leads to an increase of $1.24/hour for women and $1.97/hour for men. Both men and women also earn more if they are in an occupation requiring authority over other workers. Because AUTHORITY was measured as a 0/1 dummy variable, the coefficients indicate that women in occupations involving authority average earnings of 43 cents/hour more than women in other occupations, and that men in occupations involving authority averaged earnings of $1.98 more than men in occupations without authority, net of other controlled factors.[6] On the other hand, % HAZARDS, the measure of physical working conditions included, showed no statistically significant effect on the pay of either men or women.

Table 3.2 Results From Regressions Predicting Male or Female Average Hourly Earnings From Sex Composition, Occupational Demands, and Industrial and Organizational Controls

Dependent Variable	Average Female Hourly Earnings	Average Male Hourly Earnings
INDEPENDENT VARIABLES		
SEX COMPOSITION		
% FEMALE	−0.002**	−0.008*
	(.039)	(.067)
JOB EVALUATION VARIABLES		
ZCOGNITIVE FACTOR[+]	1.235**	1.972**
	(.000)	(.000)
AUTHORITY	0.431**	1.978**
(Dummy 1=Supervisory)	(.000)	(.000)
% HAZARDS	−0.000	−0.004
	(.971)	(.294)
CONTROL VARIABLES		
% UNION	0.017**	0.022**
	(.000)	(.001)
% GOVT	−0.002	−0.016**
	(.339)	(.006)
% SELF-EMPLOYED	−0.012**	0.019
	(.012)	(.105)
ZINDUS CAP INTENS[+]	−0.089**	0.230**
	(.006)	(.009)
ZINDUS OLIGOPOLY[+]	0.286**	0.283**
	(.000)	(.015)
ZINDUS FOR DIVIDENDS[+]	0.144**	0.069
	(.021)	(.597)
ZINDUS SALES TO GOVT[+]	−0.083	0.146
	(.113)	(.118)
ZINDUS SALES PER WKR[+]	0.055	0.120
	(.144)	(.148)
ZINDUS PROFITS[+]	−0.242**	0.107
	(.000)	(.217)
ZINDUS SALES PER FIRM[+]	−0.108**	−0.179**
	(.003)	(.050)
Intercept	5.268	7.821
R^2	.84	.73
N	403	403

* Significant on a one-tailed test at the .05 level, or on a two-tailed test at the .10 level.
** Significant on a one-tailed test at the .025 level, or on a two-tailed test at the .05 level.
[+] These variables were transformed to standardized (Z) scores before being entered into the equation.
NOTE: Numbers are regression coefficients. Probability of t statistic on two-tailed test in parentheses.

Industrial and Organizational Control Variables

Turning to the industrial and organization variables serving as controls, there were three that have the same sign and were significant for both sexes. The percentage of workers in an occupation who are unionized (% UNION) and the percent of all sales in the industry which go to the top eight firms (ZINDUS OLIGOPOLY) have positive effects. The effect of % UNION is such that for each 1 percent increase in % UNION there was a corresponding increase of about 2 cents/hour for both women and men. For ZINDUS OLIGOPOLY, each standard deviation increase led to an increase of 28-29 cents/hour for women and men. Average dollars of sales per firm (ZINDUS SALES PER FIRM) has significant and negative effects for both women and men; each standard deviation increase leads to a decrease of about 11 cents/hour for women and about 18 cents/hour for men.

The coefficients on % GOVT and % SELF-EMPLOYED suggest that both men and women earn more when they work in occupations in which more incumbents work in the private sector. The % GOVT has a negative coefficient for both sexes, although the effect is significant for men only. The % SELF-EMPLOYED has a significantly negative effect on women's earnings but a nonsignificant positive effect for men.

Many of the industrial variables have nonsignificant effects for one or both sexes. This is surprising at first glance, since past research on industrial segmentation has found effects of many of these. However, what are entered here are occupational averages for industrial variables; we would expect such effects to be weaker. Different effects for men and women probably result from men and women's different occupational placements within types of industries. While some of the effects of these variables do not have intuitive explanations, the benefit of including the variables in our model is to serve as control variables.

Sex Composition Effects: Gender Bias

Our major interest is in whether those who work in predominantly female occupations earn less than members of their own sex who work in occupations with more males, after adjustments for comparability of the occupations on the job evaluation and other control variables. The coefficients on % FEMALE answer this question in the affirmative. The coefficients of −.002 for women and −.008 for men indicate that for each additional 1 percent female in an occupation, pay goes down by .2 cents for women and .8 cents for men. At first glance this sounds trivial in magnitude. However, this implies that a woman who moved from a job that was 0% female to a job that was 100% female would lose 20 cents/hour, and a man making the same move would lose 80 cents/hour. Mean earnings of full-time year-round workers across all 403 occupations were $5.18 for women and $8.68 for men. In this context, these effects of sex composition are not trivial. If a man were to move from a job that was 100% female to a job that was 0% female, the gain of 80 cents/hour would be a pay increase of nearly 10% of what the average man earns.[7]

A few concrete examples may help to illustrate the findings about the penalty for men of being in a female, as compared to a comparable male, occupation. For this illustration, we used a regression model exactly like that in Table 3.2, except omitting the variable % FEMALE to generate a predicted wage for men in each of several well-known occupations.[8] The predicted wage is computed by substituting the scores of these occupations on the independent variables into the regression equation model. Then we compare the actual average pay of men in each of these occupations to these predicted scores. The negative coefficient on % FEMALE in the equation in Table 3.2, discussed above, indicates that, on average, female occupations pay men less than this predicted score, while male occupations pay more than this predicted score, on average. The examples below show this pattern.

Let us first consider some predominantly female occupations. Childcare workers who do not work in private homes are 89% female. Based on the regression equation from the analysis, excluding % FEMALE, we predict men in this occupation to earn $8.20/hour. Actually, they average only $4.52/hour. Registered nurses are 95% female. The regression predicts that male RNs would earn $9.96/hour, but their actual pay is only $8.47. The male regression predicts that librarians (78% female) would earn $10.31/hour, when in fact men in this occupation average only $8.26. In all these cases of predominantly female occupations, the actual amount earned by men in the jobs is less than that predicted by the regression analysis of male earnings regressed upon job evaluation variables and industrial and organizational controls.

By way of contrast, let us consider the predicted and actual pay for men in some predominantly male occupations. Consider dentists, who are only 5% female. The male regression predicts this occupation would pay $13.99/hour, but male dentists actually average $20.99/hour. Civil engineers (only 2% female) have a predicted pay of $10.77, but actual average pay of $11.77. Looking at a blue-collar male occupation, butchers and meat cutters (9% female) have a predicted wage of $6.68/hour, but actual earnings of $7.16. Thus, for all these predominantly male occupations, men earn more than the job-evaluation-based predicted earnings. While there are exceptions, the negative coefficient on % FEMALE in Table 3.2 tells us that this is the general pattern.

Women earn less than men in every occupation for reasons we do not explore here.[9] (That this is true on the average is shown by the higher intercept for the male equation.) If we take a ratio of women's mean earnings over men's mean earnings within each occupation, the average across all occupations of these ratios is .68, indicating that in the average occupation women earn 68% of what men do. (By comparison the overall ratio of women's to men's earnings was .58. This ratio is less—and therefore the sex gap is larger—overall than within occupations precisely because some of the sex gap in pay comes from between-occupational differences, from occupational segregation.)

The tendency of men to rise to the top of female occupations is documented in other chapters in this volume. But is the ratio of women's to men's earnings lower—indicating a greater within-occupation sex gap in pay—within occupations with a higher than those with a lower % FEMALE? That is, is the extent to which men earn more than women *within* occupations greater in predominantly female than in predominantly male occupations? To answer this, we ran a regression containing the same independent variables as the models in Table 3.2, but with the ratio of (full-time, year-round) women's to men's average hourly pay within the occupation as the dependent variable. The regression was weighted by the total number of persons in the occupation. The results show that the ratio of women's to men's pay is significantly smaller in occupations with a higher % FEMALE. The coefficient on % FEMALE, −.0006, shows that moving from an occupation with a % FEMALE of 0 to an occupation with a % FEMALE of 100 would decrease this ratio by .06 (6 percentage points). Since a smaller female-to-male earnings ratio within the occupation indicates a larger sex gap in pay within the occupation, this tells us that the sex gap in pay is larger within "female" than "male" occupations. However, this tendency of men to rise to the top (earnings-wise) of female occupations does not raise men's earnings enough to offset the entirety of the penalty that men suffer *relative to other men* for working in a female occupation rather than a comparable male occupation.

Conclusions

Comparable worth has been championed as a reform that would help close the portion of the sex gap in pay resulting from the devaluation of female occupations because of their sex label. Since a higher proportion of women than men are in female jobs, such a reform would improve the pay of women relative to men. Yet this should not obscure the fact that those men in female occupations are also victims of the discrimination at issue in comparable worth. This is true despite the fact that men in female jobs are simultaneously the beneficiaries of processes that lead them to rise to the top of female occupations to a greater extent than they do in male occupations. The low pay of female jobs is theorized in useful ways by cultural feminist theory. However, sociologists have much yet to contribute to our understanding of the mechanisms by which the relatively low rewards for female roles are perpetuated.

Notes

1. Two studies, Parcel, 1989, and England, 1992, found a negative effect of percent female on men's wages, but it was not statistically significant. However, since the units of analysis were *all* occupations, rather than a sample, using significance tests may be overly conservative.

2. This is based on the following calculation. The difference between the percent female of the occupation the average man and woman are in is multiplied times the regression coefficient for occupational percent female, and this product is taken as a ratio of the overall sex gap in pay. Estimates vary by what control variables were included, and whether the male or female coefficients, or a weighted average, are used. See Sorensen, 1989. For more discussion of methods of regression decomposition, see England, 1992, Chapter 3, and Jones and Kelley, 1984.

3. Others use the term *cultural feminism* differently. For example, Echols (1983) and Alcoff (1988) use it to refer to a kind of feminism that valorizes traditionally female activities and sees women's emphasis on nurturing as innate or essential to being a woman. We do not include essentialism in our definition of cultural feminism. We also do not imply by the use of the term *cultural* that this is an *ideal* rather than *materialist* theory, and see any attempt to construct this as an either/or theoretical choice as false. Materially based male power is undoubtedly one reason men succeed in getting their roles defined as more valuable and rewarded. But men's material resources are also, in part, a *result* of men's roles being socially defined as more valuable. We expect that material and ideal phenomena affect each other reciprocally. Our point in labeling the perspective *cultural* is to emphasize the role of the *devaluation* of activities typically done by women in generating gender inequality.

4. Across all 503 occupations, average male earnings are $8.59 and average female earnings $5.20, with a pay gap of $3.39 per hour. The sex gap in pay across these 403 occupations is very similar, $3.50 per hour. Although missing values led to a loss of almost 20% of the occupations, this only entailed a loss of 10% of the full-time year-round labor force since the missing occupations employed fewer people on average. A nearly identical proportion of the labor force was lost for men and women.

5. Means and standard deviations for creating normalized scores were created across occupations weighted by their total number of full-time year-round incumbents.

6. The male coefficient is significantly larger than the female coefficient for both the cognitive factor and authority.

7. The fact that the penalty for being in a predominantly female occupation is greater for men than for women is intriguing. However, we should not interpret too heavily on this difference between the male and female coefficients on percent female, since a test of statistical significance shows them not to be significantly different.

8. The coefficients from this model are very similar to those in Table 3.2.

9. The major factors explaining these within-occupation differences are probably (a) women's fewer years of employment experience and (b) job segregation such that women are in the lower-paying, more-detailed job categories within each of these occupational categories. The failure of firms to pay men and women with the same seniority equally within their most detailed job categories is also a possibility; however, we believe that this type of discrimination (prohibited by Title VII and the Equal Pay Act of 1963) is much less common than is the discrimination in placement generating segregation and the discrimination in wage setting at issue in comparable worth.

References

Acker, J. (1989). *Doing comparable worth: Gender, class and pay equity.* Philadelphia: Temple University Press.

Alcoff, L. (1988). Cultural feminism versus post-structuralism: The identity crisis in feminist theory. *Signs, 13,* 405-436.

Aldrich, M., & Buchele, R. (1986). *The economics of comparable worth.* Boston: Ballanger.

Baron, J., & Newman, A. (in press). For what it's worth: Organizational and occupational factors affecting the value of work done by women and nonwhites. *American Sociological Review.*

Beck, E. M., Horan, P. M., & Tolbert, C. M., II. (1978). Stratification in a dual economy: A sectoral model of earnings determination. *American Sociological Review, 43,* 704-720.

Chodorow, N. (1978). *The reproduction of mothering.* Berkeley: University of California Press.

Coverdill, J. E. (1988). The dual economy and sex differences in earnings. *Social Forces, 66*(4), 970-993.

Donovan, J. (1985). *Feminist theory: The intellectual traditions of American feminism.* New York: Frederick Ungar.

Echols, A. (1983). The new feminism of yin and yang. In A. Snitow, C. Stansell, & S. Thompson (Eds.), *Powers of desire: The politics of sexuality* (pp. 439-459). New York: Monthly Review Press.

Eisler, R. (1987). *The chalice & the blade: Our history, our future*. New York: Harper & Row.

England, P. (1992). *Comparable worth: Theories and evidence*. Hawthorne, NY: Aldine.

England, P., Chassie, M., & McCormick, L. (1982). Skill demands and earnings in female and male occupations. *Sociology and Social Research, 66*, 147-168.

England, P., Farkas, G., Kilbourne, B. S., & Dou, T. (1988). Explaining occupational sex segregation and wages: Findings from a model with fixed effects. *American Sociological Review, 53*, 544-558.

England, P., & McLaughlin, S. (1979). Sex segregation of jobs and male-female income differentials. In R. Alvarez, K. Lutterman, & Associates (Eds.), *Discrimination in organizations* (pp. 189-213). San Francisco: Jossey-Bass.

Farkas, G., England, P., & Barton, M. (1988). Structural effects on wages: Sociological and economic views. In G. Farkas & P. England (Eds.), *Industries, firms, and jobs: Sociological and economic approaches* (pp. 93-112). New York: Plenum.

Ferber, M. A., & Lowry, H. M. (1976). The sex differential in earnings: A reappraisal. *Industrial and Labor Relations Review, 29*, 377-387.

Filer, R. K. (1989). Occupational segregation compensating differentials and comparable worth. In R. T. Michael, H. I. Hartmann, & B. O'Farrell (Eds.), *Pay equity: Empirical inquiries* (pp. 153-170). Washington, DC: National Academy Press.

Gilligan, C. (1982). *In a different voice: Psychological theory and women's development*. Cambridge, MA: Harvard University Press.

Hartmann, H. (1976). Capitalism, patriarchy and job segregation by sex. In M. Blaxall & B. Reagan (Eds.), *Women and the workplace: The implications of occupational segregation* (pp. 137-170). Chicago: University of Chicago Press.

Hodson, R. (1983). *Workers' earnings and corporate economic structure*. New York: Academic Press.

Jaggar, A. M. (1983). *Feminist politics and human nature*. Totowa, NJ: Rowman & Allanheld.

James, S., & Dalla Costa, M. (1973). *The power of women and the subversion of the community*. Bristol, UK: Falling Wall Press.

Johnson, G., & Solon, G. (1986). Estimates of the direct effects of comparable worth policy. *The American Economic Review, 76*(5), 1117-1125.

Jones, F. L., & Kelley, J. (1984). Decomposing differences between groups: A cautionary note on measuring discrimination. *Sociological Methods & Research, 12*, 323-343.

Kalleberg, A., Wallace, M., & Althauser, R. (1981). Economic segmentation, worker power, and income inequality. *American Journal of Sociology, 87*, 651-683.

Keller, C. (1986). *From a broken web: Separation, sexism, and self*. Boston: Beacon.

Keller, E. F. (198). *Reflections on gender and science*. New Haven, CT: Yale University Press.

Kittay, E. F., & Myers, D. T. (1987). *Women and moral theory*. Totowa, NJ: Rowman and Littlefield.

Kokkelenberg, E. C., & Sockell, D. R. (1985). Union membership in the United States, 1973-1981. *Industrial and Labor Relations Review, 38*, 497-543.

O'Neill, J. (1983). *The determinants and wage effects of occupational segregation* (Urban Institute Working Paper). Washington, DC: Urban Institute.

Orazem, P., & Mattila, P. (1989). Comparable worth and the structure of earnings: The Iowa case. In R. Michael, H. Hartmann, & B. O'Farrell (Eds.), *Pay equity: Empirical inquiries* (pp. 179-199). Washington, DC: National Academy Press.

Parcel, T. (1989). Comparable worth, occupational labor markets, and occupational earnings: Results from the 1980 census. In R. Michael, H. Hartmann, & B. O'Farrell (Eds.), *Pay equity: Empirical inquiries* (pp. 134-152). Washington, DC: National Academy Press.

Parsons, T. (1954). *Essays in sociology theory* (rev. ed.). Glencoe, IL: Free Press.

Pfeffer, J., & Davis-Blake, A. (1987). The effect of the proportion of women on salaries: The case of college administrators. *Administrative Science Quarterly, 32,* 1-24.

Remick, H. (1984). Major issues in a priori applications. In H. Remick (Ed.), *Comparable worth and wage discrimination* (pp. 99-117). Philadelphia: Temple University Press.

Reskin, B. F., & Roos, P. (1990). *Job queues, gender queues: Explaining women's inroads into male occupations.* Philadelphia: Temple University Press.

Rothchild, N. (1984). Overview of pay initiatives, 1974-1984. In U.S. Commission on Civil Rights (Ed.), *U.S. commission on civil rights. Comparable worth: Issues for the 80's* (pp. 119-128). Washington, DC: Government Printing Office.

Schott, R. M. (1988). *Cognition and eros: A critique of the Kantian paradigm.* Boston: Beacon.

Shelton, B. A., & Agger, B. (1993). Shotgun wedding, unhappy marriage, no-fault divorce? Rethinking the feminism-Marxism relationship. In P. England (Ed.), *Theory on gender/Feminism on theory* (pp. 25-41). Hawthorne, NY: Aldine.

Sorensen, E. (1984). Equal pay for comparable worth: A policy for eliminating the undervaluation of women's work. *Journal of Economic Issues, 18,* 465-472.

Sorensen, E. (1989). The wage effects of occupational sex composition: A review and new findings. In M. A. Hill & M. Killingsworth (Eds.), *Comparable worth: Analyses and evidence* (pp. 57-79). Ithaca, NY: ILR Press.

Starhawk. (1987). *Truth or dare: Encounters with power, authority, and mystery.* San Francisco: Harper & Row.

Steinberg, R. J., & Haignere, L. (1987). Equitable compensation: Methodological criteria for comparable worth. In C. Bose & G. Spitze (Eds.), *Ingredients for women's employment policy* (pp. 157-182). Albany: State University of New York Press.

Steinberg, R. J., Haignere, L., Possin, C., Chertos, C. H., & Treiman, K. (1986). *The New York State pay equity study: A research report.* Albany: Center for Women in Government, State University of New York Press.

Treiman, D., & Terrell, K. (1975). Women, work and wages—Trends in the female occupational structure since 1940. In K. C. Land & S. Spilerman (Eds.), *Social indicator models* (pp. 157-200). New York: Russell Sage Foundation.

Tuana, N. (in press). *The misbegotten man: Scientific, religious, and philosophical images of woman's nature.* Bloomington: University of Indiana Press.

U.S. Department of Labor. (1977). *Dictionary of occupational titles* (4th ed.). Washington, DC: Government Printing Office.

Vogel, L. (1983). *Marxism and the oppression of women: Towards unitary theory.* New Brunswick, NJ: Rutgers University Press.

4

Men in Female-Dominated Fields

Trends and Turnover

JERRY A. JACOBS

The occupational structure of the United States, along with that of other industrialized countries, remains highly segregated by sex. In 1986 nearly 6 in 10 employed women would have had to switch occupations to be fully integrated with their male counterparts (Jacobs, 1989a, 1989b). A complementary description is equally true: 6 in 10 men would have had to change occupations to be distributed in the same manner as women. Segregation declined slowly but steadily during the 1970s and 1980s.

Most studies of occupational segregation have focused on women's exclusion from male-dominated fields, for a number of good reasons. First, jobs in male-dominated occupations offer more pay, fringe benefits, authority, and autonomy than jobs in female-dominated fields (Adelman, 1991; Bergmann, 1986; England & McCreary, 1987; Jacobs & Steinberg, 1990; Reskin, 1984; Reskin & Roos, 1990). Access to male-dominated fields seems essential for women's economic and social advancement. Second, many more fields are male-dominated than are female-dominated (Jacobs, 1989a; see also Table 4.1).[1] Consequently, the constraints imposed by sex segregation are more restrictive for women than for men. Finally, it is assumed that men would have little reason to choose female-dominated jobs when more financially rewarding alternatives are available. A simple economic explanation might seem sufficient. Thus, the processes that reduce the number of women in male-dominated fields appear to beg for explanation more urgently than the complementary limitations on men in female-dominated fields.

49

Nonetheless, an examination of the processes that divert men from pursuing female-dominated fields may well be instructive. Some evidence suggests that men employed in female-dominated occupations suffer a "prestige penalty," which parallels a similar pattern observed for women in male-dominated fields (Jacobs & Powell, 1984). This evidence suggests that male avoidance of female-dominated occupations may not simply reflect pecuniary considerations but powerful social pressures as well.

Second, it should be noted that the sex segregation of occupations does impose costs on some men, albeit far fewer than on women. An unemployed man would be better off financially if he were employed in a female-dominated occupation, yet the sex-segregated occupational structure makes this unlikely. During periods of high unemployment, gender boundaries persist, and unemployed men do not readily displace employed women in the labor market. Indeed, labor force statistics indicate that men and women have similar unemployment rates during both tight and slack labor markets (Rubery, 1988). This pattern is consistent with the existence of social barriers to men's entrance to female-dominated fields which lead them to forego the short-term economic benefits of such employment.

This chapter examines the career aspirations and occupational experiences of young men. It explores whether the revolving door pattern of mobility that has characterized women's entry into sex-atypical jobs also pertains to men's experiences in female-dominated fields. This chapter draws on extensive longitudinal and cross-sectional analyses conducted by the author (Jacobs, 1989a). I describe recent trends in men's employment before turning to data on the timing of entries and exits by men into female-dominated fields. I begin by discussing the lifelong social control processes responsible for maintaining a sex-segregated work force.

Sex Segregation and Women's Careers

A comprehensive theory of inequality must account for the way structures of inequality are reproduced. One way to address this question is to study how the sex segregation of occupations interfaces with the careers of individual women and men. Do the vast majority of women who start out working in female-dominated occupations remain employed in such settings? If so, this behavior might be due to socialization, the learned preference for such behavior. Or it might be due to rational calculations of women who intend to maximize their lifelong incomes by choosing occupations that start out with high pay and have the smallest costs associated with career interruptions. Or it might be due to discrimination from employers, which makes movement into male-dominated occupations exceptionally difficult.

Advocates of each of these theories generally assume that few women or men move between male-dominated and female-dominated fields. In other words, social psychological, human capital, and labor market discrimination theories generally assume that most women spend their entire working lives in female-dominated fields. The few women who work in male-dominated occupations are assumed to be the exceptions, different as a result of values, investments, or luck.

Let us consider the social psychological perspective in a bit more detail. I critically assessed this approach by following the occupational aspirations and subsequent labor market experiences of a group of young women. It is well documented that young men and women do aspire to different occupations: The degree of sex segregation among career goals in 1970 roughly mirrored that found in the labor force, although segregation has since declined much more rapidly in men's and women's aspirations than in the labor market itself. However, there is enormous change over time in the sex-type of occupational goals: Eighty percent of the young women surveyed changed their goals, and for this group there was virtually no relationship between the sex-type of initial goal and the sex-type of subsequent goal. Similarly, few women actually entered the occupation to which they aspired; and among those who deviated from their stated intentions, there was no relationship between the sex-type of intended occupation and the sex-type of first job. Furthermore, while I expected to find clearly demarcated barriers to women's occupational mobility, I repeatedly found a surprising amount of movement among male-dominated, sex-neutral, and female-dominated occupations. In fact, career destinations appeared to be essentially independent of the sex-type of occupational origins.

Sex segregation is reproduced at each of a number of different career stages. The structure of sex segregation remained roughly constant, but within this structure men and women moved back and forth with remarkable frequency. Women, and to a lesser extent men, played a game of musical chairs within a fixed set of sex-typed occupations. I decided to call this a "revolving door" pattern of mobility to underscore the observation that women's movement into men's occupations was often a temporary event: A high proportion of women employed in male-dominated occupations at one point or another left to enter either sex-neutral or female-dominated occupations.

What I mean by a revolving door may become more clear by contrasting it with the more familiar cumulative disadvantage view. This latter model holds that barriers loom large for girls and grow more formidable for them when they mature into women. Sex-typed socialization poses an initial set of limitations on young women's career options; sex-typed education follows, and discrimination in hiring makes matters even worse. A cumulative disadvantage model implies several specific predictions regarding sex segregation. First, older women should be more segregated from men than younger women; second, changes should be due principally to new cohorts of women entering male-dominated fields; and third, mobility patterns should reflect no mobility into male-dominated occupations, only movement out of such occupations. Yet for each of these predictions I find contrary evidence. Sex segregation has been similar at all age levels. There have been similar declines in sex segregation among each age cohort between 1970 and 1980. In other words, women already in the labor force have moved toward male-dominated fields nearly as much as new female entrants to the labor force. The same sensitivity to contemporary influences is evident among women in the formation of career aspirations and in the choices of college major. Finally, career mobility is not simply movement out of male-dominated fields, but also involves significant movement into such occupations. This evidence clearly indicates that there is no single final barrier to opportunity for women. When social restrictions on entry into male-dominated pursuits become somewhat more relaxed, some women in all age groups take advantage of these new opportunities.

In each way, then, I find that cumulative disadvantage is less consistent with the data than a revolving door pattern. Revolving doors is a lifelong process with noncumulative results.[2] Women are subject to a lifelong system of social control that continually channels and rechannels them into female-dominated fields. The question I address here is whether the same patterns may be observed for men in female-dominated fields.

The first specific item to be addressed is whether men have entered female-dominated occupations in increasing numbers in recent years. During the 1970s and 1980s, women aspired to careers in previously male-dominated fields and entered such occupations in record numbers. This analysis will thus indicate whether the decline in sex segregation involved symmetrical changes among both types of sex-typed jobs, female-dominated as well as male-dominated. The second specific question examined here is the durability of men's choices of female-dominated occupations. Do men who express a preference for working in female-dominated occupations hold this goal as an enduring commitment or as a momentary caprice? Similarly, do men employed in female-dominated fields remain in such jobs or switch back into male-dominated occupations? These questions may be addressed by following the preferences and pursuits of a group of men over a period of years.

Trends in Men's Employment
in Female-Dominated Fields

National statistics on the sex segregation of the civilian labor force in 1970 and 1980 are presented on Table 4.1. The results are derived from data in the 1970 and 1980 U.S. Censuses. These data employed the same (1980) census occupational classification system for both years, which greatly facilitates comparisons. A number of striking patterns should be noted. First, far fewer occupations are dominated by women than by men. If we defined female-dominated occupations as those in which 70% or more women are employed, and male-dominated occupations as those with 30% or fewer women employed, we find that fewer than one in six occupations is dominated by women, while in 1980 more than half of the census detailed occupations were dominated by men. (While this result is partly due to the fact that women comprise less than half of the labor force, appropriate adjustments for this fact do not change the substantive result.)

A second notable finding is that men are less likely to be employed in sex-atypical fields than women. In 1980 women were more than twice as likely to be employed in male-dominated fields as men were to be employed in female-dominated fields.

Third, women have made more progress in entering male-dominated preserves than men have in entering traditionally female enclaves. This result can be seen in several ways in Table 4.1. The number of male-dominated occupations declined substantially between 1970 and 1980, from 308 to 266. Thus, in 42 cases, occupations with less than 30% women shifted into the sex-neutral group, that is, they became occupations with 30% to 70% women. Because of this shift in the classification of the occupations themselves, the shifts in the distribution of men and women are somewhat obscured. The final column of Table 4.1 displays the 1980 employment

Table 4.1 Occupational Sex Composition, 1970 and 1980*

	1970	Men 1980 Pct. in Labor Force (N of Occupations)	1980+
male-dominated occupations 0%-29.9% female	81.21 (308)	71.24 (266)	79.98 (308)
sex-neutral occupations 30%-69.9% female	13.05 (98)	22.48 (142)	14.75 (98)
female-dominated occupations (70%-100% female)	5.74 (77)	6.28 (75)	6.27 (77)

	1970	Women 1980 Pct. in Labor Force (N of Occupations)	1980+
male-dominated occupations 0%-29.9% female	14.44 (308)	14.03 (266)	20.88 (308)
sex-neutral occupations 30%-69.9% female	20.63 (98)	27.93 (142)	22.11 (98)
female-dominated occupations (70%-100% female)	64.93 (77)	58.04 (75)	57.01 (77)

* The 1980 Census Occupational Classifications are employed for both years. (1970 data are based on a special tabulation that was coded for 1980 codes.)
+ Holds classification of occupations into sex-type categories constant at 1970 levels.

figures while maintaining the 1970 alignment of occupations. This analysis reveals that women's entrance into previously male-dominated occupations climbed to nearly 1 employed woman in 5, while only 1 employed man in 15 was employed in a previously female-dominated field.

Comparing the first and third columns indicates that the occupations shifted, not the men. When the occupations are kept in their initial slots, the distribution of men across these categories hardly changed at all. The shift evident in the second column indicates that nearly 10% of men worked in occupations that tipped over from less than 30% female to more than 30% female. As far as the women are concerned, there would have been a 6% increase in the proportion of women working in male-dominated fields, had the occupations themselves not shifted due to an increase in women's labor force participation. The result of this change was that the increase appears in the sex-neutral category rather than in the male-dominated category.

Stability and Change in Men's Aspirations and Occupations

Let us now turn to a more detailed examination of these trends in the lives of a cohort of young men and women who entered the labor force during the late 1960s and early 1970s. A group of more than 10,000 young men and women has been surveyed repeatedly since that time, providing us a unique window on changes in preferences as well as in behavior. These data were culled from the National Longitudinal Surveys (NLS) initiated by Herbert Parnes (see Jacobs, 1989a, for more details).

Career aspirations have changed more for women than for men when change is measured in terms of the sex-type of desired occupation. The proportion of young men aspiring to female-dominated fields did not rise, while during the same period the proportion of women aspiring to male-dominated fields increased substantially. The data on Table 4.2 indicate that by the end of the 1970s, women aspired to substantially more male-dominated fields than they had 10 or 12 years earlier. In contrast, men's aspirations, measured in terms of their sex composition, remained relatively constant.[3, 4] One would like more recent data on aspirations to further explore this issue; unfortunately, the panel surveys currently in progress do not include sufficiently detailed aspiration questions to allow for comparable analyses.

The sex-type of career aspirations remained quite constant for men during their teens and twenties, while for women during the same period, there was a distinct shift toward more male-dominated fields. Table 4.3 presents a more detailed breakdown of the sex-type of occupations to which young men aspired. The data indicate the remarkably small proportion of men who aspired to fields with 70% or more women. Whereas the majority of women aspired to such occupations in 1970 (more than 40% continued to designate these fields by 1980), only 2% to 4% of men aspired to such employment. In contrast, approximately 80% of men aspired to be employed in male-dominated occupations (those with less than 30%

Table 4.2 Comparison of Average Percent Female of Aspirations and Average Percent Female in Occupations, NLS Young Women and Young Men in the Labor Force

A. Women

	Aspirations Average Percent Female	Occupations Average Percent Female	N of Cases
1968	68.6	71.3	689
1969	70.8	70.8	1107
1970	68.2	72.0	1234
1971	67.2	69.8	1320
1972	66.7	70.6	1389
1973	65.8	69.4	1413
1975	64.2	67.5	1654
1977	59.0	63.8	1605
1978	58.5	63.5	1674
1980	58.0	62.6	1511

B. Men

	Aspirations Average Percent Female	Occupations Average Percent Female	N of Cases
1966	17.5	23.6	2866
1967	18.0	23.6	3390
1968	18.2	22.9	2946
1969	18.8	22.7	2875
1970	19.2	22.2	2871
1971	18.6	21.0	3061
1973	18.4	20.5	2402
1975	18.7	20.3	2402

women). These figures show no marked age trend; the small year-to-year fluctuations dwarf any age shifts in these data.

More young men are employed in female-dominated occupations than aspired to such jobs. While many individuals are not employed in the field of their choice, it is notable that in the aggregate, men's employment in sex-atypical jobs consistently exceeds the comparable aspiration measures. Overall, men move to slightly more male-dominated fields during the early stages of their careers. Some of this change is due to young men working in stopgap jobs with significant proportions of women employed before they settle into a career (Oppenheimer, 1990). By age 30 there is a closer aggregate correspondence between choices and employment.[5] In the aggregate, the sex-type of men's employment remained more constant by age than that of women.

The issue of continuity and change among individual experiences is considered in Table 4.4. The first panel of Table 4.4 presents correlations between the sex-type of career choices and outcomes at 5-year intervals for the NLS young men ages 14 to 24 in 1966. The first column reports the correlation on the durability of aspirations. The second indicates the connection between aspirations and occupational outcomes 5 years later, while the third column indicates the relationship between occupational pursuits over a 5-year period. The measure of stability is a *serial sex-type correlation,* that is, the extent to which the sex-composition (of a career aspiration or occupation) at one point in time is related to the same measure at a subsequent point in time. The second portion of Table 4.4 rearranges the same data, this time presenting the correlations in terms of specific ages. Thus, the relationship between the sex-type of choices at age 15 and age 20 is presented to indicate how well preferences at age 15 predict preferences at age 20. Similarly, the connections between ages 20 and 25 and 24 and 29 are presented.

Despite the aggregate stability just described in Table 4.3, the sex-type aspiration correlations for men presented in Table 4.4 were very low, but were slightly higher than for women. Overall, young men's aspirations at one point in time are only weak predictors of their aspirations 5 years later. Among the overwhelming majority who change their aspirations at one point or another (the row labeled "occupational changers" in Table 4.4), the sex-type correlation is only slightly positive. In other words, there is little evidence that young men's preferences for male-dominated or female-dominated occupations are firmly fixed early in life. Those who aspired to a female-dominated occupation were not much more likely than chance to prefer the same type of occupation 9 years later.

Despite the aggregate stability of sex-type of men's occupations—over time and throughout their early careers—the temporal stability of such behavior for individual men is remarkably low. In other words, men frequently change the sex-type of their jobs, despite the persistence of a highly sex-segregated occupational structure. The evidence in Table 4.4 indicates the correlation between previous and subsequent

Table 4.3 Sex-Type of Aspirations and Occupations, by Age, NLS Young Men in the Labor Force, 1966-1975

A. Aspirations

Age	Average Percent Female	Female-Dominated Occupations (70%-100% Female)	Sex-Neutral Occupations (30%-69.9% Female)	Male-Dominated Occupations (0%-29.9% Female)	N of Cases
15	15.3	1.6	19.0	79.4	1013
16	15.9	2.6	18.4	79.0	1593
17	17.6	3.3	19.5	77.2	1994
18	19.7	3.7	22.2	74.1	2211
19	20.3	3.5	22.0	74.5	2219
20	19.3	2.9	20.7	76.4	1887
21	19.9	2.8	21.1	76.1	2154
22	19.6	3.4	20.0	76.6	2027
23	18.5	2.7	19.3	78.0	2438
24	18.3	3.0	17.8	79.2	2336
25	18.2	2.3	19.1	78.6	2020
26	17.1	2.3	17.0	80.7	1697
27	17.4	2.6	16.5	80.9	1371
28	17.1	2.1	16.1	81.8	1000
29	16.8	1.8	17.5	80.7	491

B. Occupations

Age	Average Percent Female	Female-Dominated Occupations (70%-100% Female)	Sex-Neutral Occupations (30%-69.9% Female)	Male-Dominated Occupations (0%-29.9% Female)	N of Cases
15	23.7	6.5	25.2	68.2	1021
16	24.2	6.2	28.5	65.3	1761
17	25.1	6.5	32.4	61.2	2315
18	24.6	6.0	39.2	60.7	2595
19	24.6	6.1	32.4	61.5	2641
20	24.2	6.1	31.6	62.3	2215
21	23.4	5.4	30.6	64.0	2534
22	23.4	5.1	30.9	64.0	2392
23	21.5	4.2	27.8	68.0	2499
24	21.6	4.3	27.3	68.4	2037
25	20.3	3.5	26.2	70.3	1697
26	19.9	3.5	24.6	71.9	1293
27	20.3	3.1	24.1	72.8	924
28	18.9	2.8	21.6	75.6	533
29	19.3	3.0	21.8	75.2	512

59

Table 4.4   Serial Correlation of the Sex Composition of Aspirations and Occupations, NLS Young Men

A. Period Analysis

	1970 Aspiration, 1975 Aspiration		1970 Aspiration, 1975 Occupation		1970 Occupation, 1975 Occupation	
All Employed	1975		1975		1975	
	$r =$	$n =$	$r =$	$n =$	$r =$	$n =$
1970	.33**	1237	.34**	2380	.37**	2784
Occupation	1975		1975		1975	
Changers	$r =$	$n =$	$r =$	$n =$	$r =$	$n =$
1970	.12**	902	.14**	1749	.12*	1870

B. Age Analysis

	Aspiration Age 15, Aspiration Age 20		Aspiration Age 15, Occupation Age 20		Occupation Age 15, Occupation Age 20	
Entire Sample	Age 20		Age 20		Age 20	
	$r =$	$n =$	$r =$	$n =$	$r =$	$n =$
Age 15	.30**	287	.17**	347	.02*	333
Aspiration	Age 20		Age 20		Age 20	
Changers	$r =$	$n =$	$r =$	$n =$	$r =$	$n =$
Age 15	.13**	234	.15**	333	-.02	311

	Aspiration Age 20, Aspiration Age 25		Aspiration Age 20, Occupation Age 25		Occupation Age 20, Occupation Age 25	
Entire Sample	Age 25		Age 25		Age 25	
	$r =$	$n =$	$r =$	$n =$	$r =$	$n =$
Age 20	.35**	677	.25**	775	.26*	901
Aspiration	Age 25		Age 25		Age 25	
Changers	$r =$	$n =$	$r =$	$n =$	$r =$	$n =$
Age 20	.15**	496	.09*	631	.09*	725

	Aspiration Age 24, Aspiration Age 29		Aspiration Age 24, Occupation Age 29		Occupation Age 24, Occupation Age 29	
Entire Sample	Age 29		Age 29		Age 29	
	$r =$	$n =$	$r =$	$n =$	$r =$	$n =$
Age 24	.49**	592	.38**	654	.41*	749
Aspiration	Age 29		Age 29		Age 29	
Changers	$r =$	$n =$	$r =$	$n =$	$r =$	$n =$
Age 24	.21**	375	.16**	464	.24*	587

$*p < .05$
$**p < .01$

sex-type of occupation is quite low, and is especially weak for the great majority of young men who change occupations at some point during the early stages of their careers. The same conclusion is reached when the data are arranged in terms of age or in terms of period. Indeed, the sex-type correlation increases only slightly as young men enter their late twenties.

Conclusions

The evidence presented here indicates both similarities and differences in recent experiences of men and women. The principal similarity between men's and women's experiences of sex segregation is that for both groups there appears to be a lifelong system of social control that continues to put social pressure to conform to gender-appropriate behavioral norms. The evidence reveals only a weak relationship between early preferences and behavior and later preferences and behavior. In other words, for men, the choice of a female-dominated field is quite uncommon and rarely endures for long; employment in female-dominated fields for men is similarly unusual and often brief.

One should keep in mind that a fundamental difference between men and women is the type of destination one enters when leaving a sex-atypical occupation. Women who leave male-dominated fields are much more likely to experience downward social mobility than are men who leave female-dominated fields. Thus, there is an important asymmetry in these patterns despite the surface-level similarity. Consequently, it may be that women are more likely to be *pushed* out of male-dominated fields while men are more likely to be *pulled* out of female-dominated fields.

One principal difference between men and women documented here is that men's pursuit of female-dominated fields is even more unusual than women's pursuit of male-dominated fields. Why are sex-atypical choices more common for women than for men? There are at least three explanations of this difference that present themselves. First, it might be that the pressures for sex-role conformity are stronger for men than for women. In short, a man accused of being a sissy may be much more vulnerable than a woman accused of trying to be macho. An alternative explanation, however, would be that men are not drawn to female-dominated occupations because they are relatively unattractive in terms of wages and benefits. A final alternative holds that this result is an artifact of the limited number of female-dominated occupations. This view holds that sex segregation is more restrictive for women because they are confined to a smaller set of occupations. Perhaps the entrance of men into this small set of fields is so unusual because relatively few fields are dominated by women. This present analysis is not able to adjudicate among these three alternatives. Further research should attempt to determine whether men are so scarce in female-dominated fields because these fields are so limited, because of greater gender-role pressure on men, or because social pressure is combined with unattractive economic prospects in these jobs.

A related point is that women have made much greater inroads into male-dominated occupations than men have into female-dominated occupations. My view is that the women's movement has done much to open up doors for women and to provide a context for wider aspirations for women. No similar social movement has challenged stereotypes for men.

The evidence does seem to suggest that there is strong resistance faced by workers who violate sex-role norms in terms of occupational choices, resulting in a revolving door pattern of mobility for both women and men. This resistance continues throughout life; it is not a simple matter of values internalized at an early age that merely "express themselves" later in life. In this sense, the case of men in female-dominated fields parallels the experience of women working in male-dominated preserves.

Notes

1. The evidence indicates that women are more concentrated in a limited number of fields than men. One interesting change in this pattern, however, is that in recent years male college freshmen's choices of major were more concentrated (principally in business and engineering) than those of their female counterparts.

2. It should be noted, however, that income patterns conform to a cumulative disadvantage pattern: Women fall further and further behind men as cohorts age.

3. Data and methods are discussed in detail in Jacobs, 1989a. The present results include additional tabulations by age, following the procedures employed in Jacobs, Karen, and McClelland, 1991.

4. The period covered by men asks for desired occupation at age 30, for women, desired occupation at age 35. The time period covered for men is somewhat shorter because the questions were not asked after 1976, when a majority of the men in the sample were age 30 or more.

5. These data by themselves do not answer the question of whether young men are actually changing fields, or whether those who start working later, after having attended college, are employed in more male-dominated fields than those who start work at an earlier age. However, other evidence (Jacobs, 1993) indicates that the employment of young men in female-dominated service fields is often temporary, with high rates of exits by men in their twenties and early thirties.

References

Adelman, C. (1991). *Women at thirtysomething: Paradoxes of attainment.* Washington, DC: U.S. Department of Education.

Bergmann, B. (1986). *The economic emergence of women.* New York: Basic Books.

England, P., & McCreary, L. (1987). Gender inequality in paid employment. In B. B. Hess & M. M. Ferree (Eds.), *Analyzing gender: A handbook of social science research* (pp. 286-321). Beverly Hills, CA: Sage.

Jacobs, J. A. (1989a). *Revolving doors: Sex segregation and women's careers.* Palo Alto, CA: Stanford University Press.

Jacobs, J. A. (1989b). Long term trends in occupational segregation by sex. *American Journal of Sociology, 95*(1), 160-173.

Jacobs, J. A. (1992). Careers in the U.S. service economy, 1969-1987. In G. Esping-Andersen (Ed.), *A post-industrial proletariat?* Newbury Park, CA: Sage.

Jacobs, J. A., Karen, D., & McClelland, K. (1991). The dynamics of young men's career aspirations. *Sociological Forum, 6*(4), 609-639.

Jacobs, J. A., & Powell, B. (1984). Gender differences in the evaluation of prestige. *Sociological Quarterly, 25*(2), 173-190.

Jacobs, J. A., & Steinberg, R. (1990). Compensating differentials and the male-female wage gap: Evidence from the New York State pay equity study. *Social Forces, 69*(2), 439-468.

Oppenheimer, V. (1990). *Life-cycle jobs and the transition to adulthood.* Unpublished paper, Department of Sociology, University of California at Los Angeles.

Reskin, B. F. (Ed.). (1984). *Sex segregation in the workplace: Trends, explanations, remedies.* Washington, DC: National Academy Press.

Reskin, B. F., & Roos, P. (Eds.). (1990). *Job queues, gender queues: Explaining women's inroads into male occupations.* Philadelphia: Temple University Press.

Rubery, J. (Ed.). (1988). *Women and recession.* London: Routledge.

5

Seekers and Finders

Male Entry and Exit in Female-Dominated Jobs

L. SUSAN WILLIAMS
WAYNE J. VILLEMEZ

After a decade of investigating women's entry into nontraditional occupations (for example, see Morrison, White, Van Velsor, & The Center
for Creative Leadership, 1987; Reskin & Roos, 1990; Stromberg &
Harkess, 1988), sociologists have turned increasingly to the study of
men as gendered workers and of ways in which gender bias is perpetuated in female occupations. While recent studies have offered insight
into the phenomenon of men in nontraditional occupations through case
studies (Hall, 1993; Leidner, 1991; Williams, 1989, 1992), little has
been done to gain systematic knowledge about male entry and exit
patterns in female-dominated occupations.

This study profiles men in female-dominated occupations and traces
the dynamics of their entry into and exit from those jobs. We examine
three groups of men: those who actively sought jobs that are female-
dominated (seekers); those who found them—including those who were
looking for other types of work (finders); and those who were in female
jobs and left them (leavers). All three groups overlap. Using data from
a large random sample of workers and employers in the Chicago SMSA,
we first look at men who actually preferred jobs in occupations dominated by women, examining individual characteristics, job-related
attitudes, and positional differences between those who successfully
located in high-percent female occupations and those who did not.
Second, we focus on men who are currently in occupations dominated

by women, differentiating between those who actively sought this kind of job and those who did not. Third, by tracing mobility patterns of men who experience various routes in and out of occupations defined by percent female, we posit a more complex depiction of economic outcome than is apparent through simpler "still shot" views of these jobs. We focus on three questions: Are social control effects different for men than for women? Do men experience similar mobility in and out of gender atypical jobs, both in degree and direction, as women do? And finally, are there analytically important distinctions among men in female jobs?

Recent occupational sex segregation literature follows two general avenues: that which views segregation as a partial outcome of both individual choice and market processes, and another view which implicates segregation as one of the causes of inequality (for a critique, see Villemez, Williams, Bridges, & Morris, 1992). The first account is informed by Jacobs's (1989) reworking of concepts of discrimination and market influence into a "social control" perspective. Jacobs argues that discriminatory actions and structures influence individual decisions about job mobility that enable impersonal market processes to at least partially explain sex segregation. Individual decisions, he argues, are regulated by social control mechanisms, which dictate expectations about the types of jobs men and women seek and remain in. This perspective generates a "revolving door" metaphor, which, for Jacobs, explains the coexistence of sex segregation and extensive mobility of females in and out of male-dominated occupations. The second emphasis is exemplified by England, Farkas, Kilbourne, and Dou (1988), who emphasize "structural niches," which operate in both labor markets and household behavior to perpetuate the concentration of women in disadvantaged jobs. Though they posit the same general framework, there is a clear difference in emphasis between the two: Jacobs stresses the frequent movement of workers in and out of sex-atypical jobs; England et al. highlight the institutional constraints, reinforced by socialization, that bar most females from entering all but "women's work." We believe both are useful foci for studying men's behavior in nontraditional jobs, but need modification to deal with important differences between males and females and between jobs defined as male-dominated and female-dominated.

Jacobs correctly identifies social control as a normative measure that both persuades and constrains individual choice of workers, and Williams (1992) further clarifies how "negative stereotypes about men who do 'women's work' can push men out of specific jobs" (p. 263). This is a useful perspective, for it is clear that social control mechanisms should both limit the number of men entering female occupations and pressure those in them to leave. In the case of men, however, we are dubious about the use of the revolving door metaphor, which may overemphasize the extent of job mobility. Even for females, Jacobs's own data show that only 10% of those in traditionally female jobs had shifted to traditionally male jobs after a 10-year period. For males, we would expect even fewer. And, as we demonstrate below, the majority of men seem to enter female-dominated occupations, not through a revolving door, but rather through a "trapdoor"—most were not seeking such entry.

Further, we do not find evidence of extensive mobility patterns across sex-segregated occupations for men. However, if one emphasizes those aspects of the social control perspective that explicitly include the construction of barriers that directly block some men from their goals—forging structures such as those identified by England—we also expand our understanding of how organizations create gender regimes (Connell, 1987) and perpetuate gender inequality. Our data, which demonstrate that many men are steered away from high-percent female jobs, support this thesis.

Theoretically, we offer a clarification of social control, based on assumptions of a gender model. We differentiate between individual-level social control, which operates normatively both directly and through group mediation, and structural social control, which emerges when individuals use gender protocol—based on hegemonic masculinity—to erect barriers and construct gender regimes which keep men out of female-defined work. Jacobs has strongly emphasized individual-level social control for females; we argue that structural control is also strongly influential for male outcomes.

At the individual level, males internalize the norms of hegemonic masculinity, which rewards the *ideals* of masculinity, regardless of its correspondence with actual traits of the majority of men (Connell, 1987). Hegemonic masculinity may preclude many men from seeking female-dominated jobs, and may also influence individuals through group-mediated sanctions that maintain work segregation and protect male dominance (Reskin, 1988). As Acker states, "Individual men and particular groups of men do not always win in these processes, but masculinity always seems to symbolize self-respect for men at the bottom and power for men at the top, while confirming for both their gender's superiority" (1990, p. 145). Men have a vested stake in maintaining the ideals of masculinity (which include "whiteness" and heterosexuality), and therefore we cannot assume social control works the same way as for women, or for all men.

Structural constraints often develop out of day-to-day activities, many of which operate differently for men in female-dominated work. For example, employers considering men who apply for women's work may dismiss an applicant as one who would not seriously seek long-term employment. Gender-based assumptions may be drawn concerning his motives or his sexual orientation. In addition, social control may generate patterns of practice, based on gendered conventions, which structure physical constraints into organizations. For instance, if a day-care center has open toilet facilities for the children (which is often the case to prevent questions of abuse), a male employee may not be seen as an appropriate caretaker in that situation; if the facilities are not open, his intentions may be even more questionable than a woman's. In either case, he may be blocked from employment—the revolving door is often locked.

Additionally, we must place the concept of social control in the context of goals and aspirations. Most research on people in nontraditional occupations has been based on assumptions surrounding women in men's jobs. Just as social control may work differently for men than for women, theory that assumes all men in women's jobs are there because they want to be leads us astray, as do data that lump together all men in female-dominated occupations. Some men may be in a high-percent female job simply because of availability or convenience. To the extent that not all men are in those jobs for the same reasons, we must use a different framework that incorporates the context of goals.

Our data enable us to distinguish between two kinds of finders, those who actively sought and found work in high-percent female jobs and those who just ended up there (via an invisible trapdoor); and between two kinds of seekers, those who sought and found female jobs and those who sought but did not find them. We also discern two mobility patterns in which female occupations affect specific groups of men who later relocate in another job—the leavers. Some men use female-dominated occupations as a fast track to success, while others stay in dead-end jobs or move to others just as disadvantageous. By identifying these more subtle forms of selection, we can isolate processes which not only advantage men over women, but which also target a very select group of men as preferred candidates over other men and clarify ways in which certain groups gain privilege over others. Specifically, we focus on possible ways in which social control affects men in sex-atypical work differently from women's experiences, including individual-level and structural constraints; characteristics and patterns of movement of men who move in and out of female-dominated jobs; and important distinctions among men in women's work—those who actually sought their work and those who fell through a trapdoor. Identifying the seekers and finders, as well as the leavers, facilitates this project.

Data and Methods

Data used in the analyses are from a 1981 survey of 2,713 workers and their employers in the Chicago SMSA.[1] The study first gathered data from individual workers, all of whom were employed for at least 20 hours per week. A large proportion of the survey instrument dealt with the job-search process, so we know the specific type of job being sought, even if a different type of job was ultimately found. Information was also collected on previous jobs, including one with a prior employer and up to two prior jobs with the current employer, yielding a possible history of four jobs per employee.

In the second stage of the study, the workers' current employers were interviewed about the job in which the sampled employee worked, including characteristics such as the typical means of recruiting and screening workers, and the starting and average salaries for workers in the specific position occupied by the employee respondent.

Jobs are classified for the purposes of this study by the percent of female workers in each six-digit occupation/industry category, available from the U.S. Census Bureau, which identifies a specific occupation in a particular industry. We utilize a quartile classification for most comparative analyses; our cut points, like those of previous researchers, are arbitrary.

Seekers are operationalized in two ways: *Successful seekers* are men who actively looked for and found a job in an occupation that is high-percent female; *redirected seekers* are those who stated they wanted a job that is high-percent female but were located elsewhere. Finders are also of two types: *premeditated finders*—the same workers as our successful seekers—who said they wanted and actively searched for a job that is high-percent female; and *diverted finders,* who did not state a preference for a female job but located in one that was high-percent female. Leavers are men who have ever held high-percent female jobs and currently do not.

We often are limited to small Ns in certain categories and therefore must make inferences with caution. However, we believe the results are meaningful because of the representativeness of the large initial sample and because of the quality of the data obtained. We have no reason to believe that the subsample, though small, is atypical.

Description of Findings

Seekers

All Seekers

We first identified those men who state that they seriously considered jobs only of a certain type (N = 477). The majority of male seekers (65%) sought sex-typical jobs (0%-25% female), and an additional 29.5% preferred mixed jobs (25%-75% female). However, 5.5% stated they earnestly desired and actively sought nontraditional jobs (75%-100% female). While the large majority of men are obviously deterred from jobs largely female, at least some "strongly prefer" work in those areas. When we determined where the seekers located, defined by percentage of females in the occupation, the data reveal that most men who seek traditional male jobs get them (82%); otherwise there is only about a 50% chance that they will successfully acquire the type of job they desire.[2] Surprisingly, a substantial number of men were apparently turned away from positions in female jobs. Of the 26 men who preferred a job that is female-dominated, only 13 actually located there—indication that some sort of control mechanism is blocking these men, despite their job preferences. Those 13 who did not were about evenly distributed among the other job types. Note that our sample contains 75 males in female jobs, but 62 of them were not actively seeking them. We discuss first the 13 of those 75 who actually sought the jobs they are in, and then the 13 who preferred female-dominated jobs, but were redirected to other occupations.

Though few in number, men who say they prefer jobs that are high-percent female share common characteristics that are different from men who seek male jobs. Men wanting specific jobs that are female-dominated are somewhat younger (34 vs. 38), slightly better educated (15 years vs. 14), have fewer years of experience (14 vs. 18), and are much less likely to be married (42% vs. 69%). They report smaller household size (2.2 vs. 2.5), lower family income ($18,574 vs.

$33,592), and despite being less often married, are nonetheless likely to be the sole contributor to family income (54% vs. 64%). More of them say they would work anywhere if the salary were high enough (58% vs. 43%). They are clearly a different group from those who actively seek male jobs. This indicates that in addition to having distinct personal desires and/or perceptions of opportunity, men who seek female jobs are in different social and structural positions than men who seek more "male" jobs, and may be prone to different types of social control.

Successful and Redirected Seekers

The above findings prompt two questions: How are men who want female jobs but do not find them different from those who do? And are unsuccessful seekers of any job a unique group? To answer these questions, we first examine differences between successful male seekers of female jobs ($n = 13$) with unsuccessful male seekers of female jobs ($n = 13$) and compare differences with those between the same categories of males who sought male jobs ($n = 254$ and $n = 55$, respectively).[3]

There is no discernible difference between successful and unsuccessful seekers of male jobs, but considerable difference between successful and unsuccessful seekers of female jobs. For those males looking for female jobs, successful seekers on average are younger than redirected seekers (31 vs. 38), less experienced (12 years vs. 14), and considerably less likely to be married (23% vs. 62%). When they locate, successful seekers are in smaller firms (8,386 vs. 27,243), are less likely to be in jobs protected from outside hiring (12% vs. 33%), and more are in positions that do not mandate college education (62% vs. 46%)—all of this in large part attributable to the fact that they are in female jobs. Successful seekers are also more likely to be supervisors (77% vs. 54%). Actually, men redirected from male jobs to mixed or female jobs also are more likely to be supervisors than men who found male jobs (64% vs. 36%), indicating both that the chance for supervisory status for men is greater in less male jobs, and that this increased chance may be part of the inducement driving the redirection process. The successful seekers are more likely to belong to unions (31% vs. 15%) and to work part time (23% vs. 15%); they also average lower tenure (3.1 years vs. 7.5 years) and report lower job satisfaction. Only 23% of successful seekers report being very satisfied, while 46% of redirected seekers do. We know that only half the men in our sample who strongly preferred a job that is female-dominated successfully located one. In addition, these data suggest that the process of success versus redirection is not a random one, but falls into a discernible pattern. Beyond individual-level social control that discourages most men from seeking female jobs, there may be structural mechanisms that systematically block the revolving door for some. This possibility warrants further examination of men who prefer female jobs, both those who successfully locate and those who do not.

Profile of Successful Seekers. For a closer look, Table 5.1A displays specific characteristics of the 13 men who successfully searched for and found female-dominated jobs. The largest single category is identified as those who have specifically trained for a traditionally female profession or semi-profession, such as elementary school teacher (n = 4), hairdresser (*n* = 2), and nurse (*n* = 1). Clerical seekers also appear successful in their job search (bank teller, file clerk, supervisor of general office), as do one sales worker and one recreation worker. Interestingly, the one male who pursued a child-care job was unsuccessful, but obtained another high-percent female job as a statistical clerk. It seems reasonable, then, that the door is open to some men who actively seek jobs in female-defined areas, but it may direct them to very specific areas of work. In addition, some domains, such as child care, may be particularly formidable to men's entry. Social control may also vary in intensity, especially when it is based on gendered traditions of nurturance, which are espoused to be "natural."

All but 3 of the men are young (19 to 31). One of the older males has taught for 20 years; the 2 others (ages 47 and 52) report low tenure (less than a year) with current employer, indicating possible career changes (the 47-year-old has just moved from a largely male occupation). Only the 3 older men are married, 2 others are divorced, and the remaining 8 have never been married. It is possible that social control mechanisms are applied more leniently toward youth. Additionally, employers may be more suspicious of the long-term motives of older applicants (and question, for example, why the older applicants are not already situated in men's work, where they also could be earning more), unless they are in a field for which they are very specifically trained, such as teaching.

Twelve of the 13 listed a previous job. Seven moved from other high-percent female occupations; one came from a "mixed" occupation (40%-60% female); and 4 came from predominantly male occupations. Except one teacher, all had been on the job 4 years or less. Only one said he was worse off than before; most said they were better off. Intriguing, though, is the fact that 5 reported earning less than they

Table 5.1A Profile of Male Successful Seekers of Female Jobs (75%-100% female)

Job Wanted (75%-100% Female)	Job Found (75%-100% Female)	Average Salary of All in Job	Tenure in Years	Job Type Previous (% Fem.)	Better Off?	Earning More?	Age	Marital Status
Teacher, Elem.	Teacher, Elem.	$16,500	4.0	10-20	yes	no	26	never
Teacher, Elem.	Teacher, Elem.	$16,500	20.0	0-10	yes	yes	48	married
Teacher, Elem.	Teacher, Elem.	$24,000	0.5	20-40	no	no	47	married
Teacher, Elem.	Teacher, Elem.	$14,725	4.0	80-90	yes	no	31	divorced
Hairdresser	Hairdresser	$ 9,751	0.6	80-90	yes	yes	26	never
Hairdresser	Hairdresser	$15,000	1.5	80-90	same	yes	28	never
Nursing	Registered Nurse	$20,620	2.0	20-40	yes	yes	28	never
Supervisor, Gen. Ofc.	Supervisor, Gen. Ofc.	$17,000	1.2	90-100	yes	yes	24	divorced
Bank Teller	Bank Teller	$13,298	0.8	40-60	yes	yes	19	never
File Clerk	File Clerk	$17,789	0.1	80-90	yes	no	52	married
Rec. Worker	Rec. Worker	$13,500	1.5	—	—	—	19	never
Sales Worker, Apparel	Sales Worker, Other Commodity	$20,468	2.0	0-10	yes	yes	26	never
Child Care	Stat. Clerk	$13,960	2.0	60-80	yes	no	26	never

would expect to be earning in their previous job, but 4 of those thought they were better off in the new job. We interpret this as evidence that at least some men are sincerely interested in the qualitative aspect of work that they find in female jobs; unfortunately, gender regimes designed on assumptions of hegemonic masculinity ignore individual goals and aspirations, even those of some men.

Profile of Redirected Seekers. Is a pattern discernible among those turned away? Table 5.1B describes male seekers of female jobs who did not find work in a female occupation, those for whom the revolving door was locked. As noted previously, the most obvious differences between the successful seekers and the redirected seekers are their age and marital status. Analyzing where and why they were blocked is more complex. While successful seekers seemed to have located well in the professions and semi-professions, some redirected seekers also wanted positions in those same occupations. Even here, though, we find strong evidence of gendered channeling. For example, 4 men listed elementary school teacher as their preference. Two of those found teaching jobs not classified as high-percent female, one in school administration and one in other administration. Those preferring clerical positions are also in related fields, but in more male jobs: Those seeking bookkeeping/clerking jobs became financial managers or accountant/auditors; one applying for sales support is in marketing management; and one looking for a management-related position found work as an accountant. Other men who wanted work in food establishments and in printing industries also found jobs in related fields. Only one worker took a position totally unrelated to his stated preference. He searched for a legal assistant position, but found work in insurance sales.

A striking fact is that in more than half the cases, the redirected male seeker found a managerial position, whereas the job he actually sought and for which he claimed a "strong preference" was not a management position. They were thus placed directly in a management position for which they did not intend to apply. And the alternative path seems to be more financially rewarding. Positions currently held by redirected seekers have an average salary of $20,492 (as reported by the employer), 25% higher than the average for positions held by successful seekers ($16,393). This evidence demonstrates how gender regimes are maintained bi-directionally both through constraints—which utilize both individual-level and structural social control—and through the "glass escalator" effect found by Williams (1992). Gender often remains faithful to its dominant group, even when individuals try to resist the "natural" flow.

Table 5.1B Profile of Male Redirected Seekers of Female Jobs (75%-100% Female)

Job Wanted (75%-100% Female)	Job Found (0%-75% Female)	Average Salary of All in Job	Tenure in Years	Job Type Current (% Fem.)	Better Off?	Earning More?	Age	Marital Status
Teacher, Elem.	Admn., Educ.	$25,410	3.0	20-40	yes	no	27	married
Teacher, Elem.	Teacher, n.e.c.	$13,500	0.8	60-80	yes	yes	30	married
Teacher, Elem.	Mgt. and Admn.	$25,410	20.0	60-80	yes	yes	42	separated
Teacher, Elem.	Teacher, Bus.	$15,000	22.0	60-80	—	—	44	married
Bookkeeper	Fin. Mgr.	$7,855	15.0	40-60	yes	yes	45	married
Bookkeeper	Fin. Mgr.	$22,712	10.0	40-60	yes	yes	38	married
Bookkeeper	Accountant	$25,410	4.0	20-40	yes	yes	29	never
Sales Support	Management	$29,067	3.0	20-40	yes	no	53	married
Waiter/ Waitress	Supervisor, Food Prep.	$8,500	6.0	40-60	no	no	34	married
Management Related, n.e.c.	Accountant and Auditor	$19,200	2.0	40-60	yes	yes	42	separated
Misc. Food Preparation	Butcher, Meat Cutter	$19,000	5.0	10-20	—	—	47	divorced
Photoengraver, Lithographer	Misc. Print Mach. Oper.	$26,000	1.0	40-60	yes	yes	27	married
Legal Assistant	Insurance Sales	$29,333	0.1	10-20	—	yes	25	never

Finders

Premeditated Finders and Diverted Finders

Though some males seeking female jobs did not find them, other males who were not seeking female jobs ended up in them—testimony to the trapdoor effect. Table 5.2 presents some interesting differences between the 13 males who deliberately sought and found female jobs, and the 62 males who found them while seeking more traditional employment. We call the former *premeditated finders* and the latter *diverted finders* (note that premeditated finders are our same successful seekers, renamed for this comparison). At the outset, it is of interest that of the 75 males in traditional female jobs, only 13 actually sought them. More than 80% fell through a trapdoor into these jobs, for reasons that are likely separate from individual goals and aspirations. While we might assume most women are in male jobs because of both individual preference and economic and status incentives, we cannot make that assumption for the large majority of men in female jobs. Clearly, most men who are in female-dominated jobs did not actively seek that employment, and they average lower wages than all other categories of men.

Compared to diverted finders, premeditated finders are quite clearly different people in different jobs, and, at least to some extent, are doing different things. A striking difference by race is noted. While all of the 13 premeditated finders are non-Hispanic white, 27% ($n = 17$) of the diverted finders (those who fall through the trapdoor) are minority.[4] Minority men in female-dominated jobs clearly exhibit a different pattern from minority women in the same occupations. While about the same proportions of men and women are minority among diverted finders (27% of men, 30% of women), 27% of successful female seekers in female jobs are classified as minority, compared to zero percent of minority men.

These differences raise interesting questions about how race and ethnicity interact with gender to manifest different meanings and behavior for individual men (cf. Messner, 1992). Others have pointed to variants of masculinity, such as exaggerated machismo among Chicanos and the "cool pose" among African-American men (Majors, 1992). There is evidence that masculinity may work differently for minority men, but not because of fundamental cultural differences in aspirations. Contradictions inherent in American hegemonic masculinity may be more visible among minority men who internalize the ideals of masculinity while being denied equal access to resources that legitimate it

Table 5.2 Males in Female Jobs (75%-100% Female): Characteristics of Premeditated Finders (Workers Who Sought and Found Female Jobs) and Diverted Finders (Workers Who Are in Female Jobs But Did Not Seek Them)

	Premeditated Finders (N = 13)	Diverted Finders (N = 62)	
		White (n = 45)	Nonwhite (n = 17)
Mean Age	30.77	38.41	32.47
% Married	23.08	46.67	29.41
Mean Years of Education	15.0	14.07	11.89
% With College Degree and More	53.84	24.45	35.29
% With Graduate Education	46.15	8.89	11.76
Mean Years of Experience	12.0	19.40	11.24
Mean Family Income Reported	$15,200	$27,194	$20,934
Mean Number in Household	1.89	2.56	3.0
% Who Are Sole Contributor	53.85	43.18	58.82
Mean Firm Size	8,386	56,657	9,076
Mean Establishment Size	534	1,801	1,144
% in Jobs With College Degree Required	38.46	22.72	25.0
% in Jobs Protected From Outside Hiring	12.50	45.45	0.0
% Respondents Who Work Part Time (>35)	23.08	22.22	23.53
% Who Belong to Unions	30.77	15.56	41.18
Mean Years of Tenure	3.1	8.6	3.3
% Respondents Who Supervise Others	76.92	44.44	41.18
Mean Score on Job Satisfaction (1 = very satisfied)	1.77	1.71	1.82

(Cazenave, 1984; Zinn, 1992). Thus, masculinity may become more salient as it takes on a greater importance for minority men who do not have access to rewards associated with more traditional jobs. Of all male seekers of gender-atypical jobs in our sample, less than 10% (n = 2) were minority; both were blocked.

These findings raise three issues. First, minority men—who are typically blocked from resources and power equal to white men—may be even more likely to preserve their traditional masculine identity by refusing women's work. Second, those minorities who do seek gender-atypical employment may be doubly deprived; race is most often a cumulative disadvantage. Third, racial and ethnic minority men, because they do not have as many legitimate employment options, have different choices. While some may turn to illegitimate alternatives and some may drop out entirely, still others may change aspirations relative to perceived opportunity. A job that does not attract them initially (because it is "women's work") becomes more "masculine" and therefore more acceptable when it affords a weekly paycheck and status as a breadwinner. A paradox emerges: Minority men may feel their identity via masculinity is more threatened through work in gender-atypical work, but nevertheless they disproportionately end up there.

Although the group of minority men (among diverted finders) averages lower education than whites, 35% have at least a college degree, suggesting two kinds of workers: those in professions with a degree requirement and those in low-level and menial labor positions. Generally, minority diverted finders are younger, average more household members but lower family income, and are employed in smaller firms than the white diverted finders. They have lower job satisfaction than either of the categories of white workers in female jobs—men may also experience affective costs when they are isolated from the "masculinizing practices" of more conventional workplaces (Connell, 1990).

To avoid confounding racial and ethnic differences with other distinctions, the remaining comparisons in this section are between premeditated finders (all white) and white diverted finders. Characteristically, premeditated finders are younger (30) than diverted finders (38), half as likely to be married (23% vs. 47%), and are better educated (15 years vs. 14). They are twice as likely to have a college degree, and among those who hold a degree, 46% of the premeditated finders have a graduate education beyond a bachelor's, while only 9% of the diverted finders do. The young men who actively sought a female job have, on average, 7 years less experience (12 vs. 19) than those who just ended up in them. The two groups have different kinds of families. The premeditated finders average 1.89 people per household, compared with 2.56 for diverted finders, and report considerably less family income ($15,200 vs. $27,194). Premeditated finders are more likely to be the sole supporter in the family unit (54% vs. 43%).

Different job characteristics indicate that they are not all in similar locations. Among the premeditated finders, 39% report college degree requirements, while only 23% of the white diverted finders do. Those males who looked for female jobs tend to find them in smaller firms (8,386) than other white males in female jobs (56,657) and in smaller establishments as well (534 vs. 1,801). Only 13% of premeditated finders report being in a sheltered job (internal labor market), while 46% of white diverted finders are in protected jobs. On the job, the two groups also differ. Premeditated finders average less tenure with current employer (3.1 vs. 8.6 years), and are twice as likely to supervise other workers (77% vs. 44%).

The premeditated finders differ in two important ways from other men in female occupations. First, although they may be in similar occupations (and a detailed analysis of occupational categories reveals they are), they appear to be there for different reasons. The premeditated finders stay a shorter time (as indicated by age, experience, and tenure), and are more likely to use the position as a vehicle to advance them to higher-status jobs (as indicated by overqualification). This suggests that while they may truly "desire" a female job, they also are likely to have perceived potential for career advancement. Some men may subvert social control mechanisms when they can justify their "use" of female jobs.

Second, premeditated finders are an occupationally concentrated group. They tend to be either professionals or clerical workers. The diverted finders, on the other hand, are more diverse, encompassing both the professions and also many jobs that accept lower-level quali-fications, such as sales workers, assemblers, packers, equipment oper-ators, and dry cleaners. Even among the professionals, the diverted finders exhibit a greater tendency to remain in female occupations. For example, earlier we showed that among seekers who wanted bookkeep-ing positions, most were "boosted" to managerial jobs; but among diverted finders, we identify 11 bookkeepers who are apparently willing to stay there, at least for an average of almost 9 years. Even within occupations, men in female-dominated jobs are not a homogeneous group.

We also identify diverted finders who obviously were blocked from other kinds of occupations, and who are probably in female jobs solely because of availability. For example, one telephone operator really wanted to drive a truck, a construction painter found work as a hand packer, and a telephone repairman/installer is now a bookkeeper. The above findings clearly demonstrate the importance of including the context of goals and aspirations. In doing so, we are able to distinguish those few who entered through the revolving door—a rather elite group who seem willing and able to circumvent both individual-level and structural-level social control—and the majority who fell through the trapdoor, a group in which at least some more likely "settled" for a female-dominated job.

Leavers

To test inferences from previous findings, which suggest that female occupations may provide a stopgap in job mobility for men, we explore another category of men, the leavers—men who have ever held high-percent female jobs and currently do not. We identified 105 males who have previously held traditionally female jobs but have moved out of those positions. Most of those leavers (75%) are currently in predominantly male occupations, demonstrating the strain toward gender consistency and the absence of a great deal of gender mobility. As additional support for the strong tendency toward sex segregation, the men in our sample who leave male jobs also find new positions in high-percent male jobs. And most female leavers of female jobs relocate in female jobs.

A comparison of men who have held high-percent female jobs (regardless of where they are now located) with men still in high-percent female jobs reveals very few differences in individual and job characteristics. One that stands out, however, is that leavers average higher on-job satisfaction and are much more likely to report being very satisfied (51% vs. 26%). They are, in fact, the highest scorers in job satisfaction among all groups we compare, while those men currently in female jobs score the lowest. Both individual-level social control, which underscores where workers should work, and structural social control, which directs employees toward gender-appropriate jobs (and which also rewards them according to gender-inspired social and economic standards), is evidenced here. Although Williams (1992) found no prejudice or discrimination against men within occupations dominated by women, the men in our sample are undoubtedly happier when they leave.

The Money Translation

The nature of the data allows us to compare the starting salary and average salary for the specific job held by the employee respondent (employer respondents provided these figures—they were asked only about specific jobs within the establishment, and were unaware that any holder of that job had been interviewed). The figure we use for earnings is the actual earnings reported by the respondent.

Table 5.3A displays the results for jobs that are at least 50% female. Percent female provides a clear continuum for starting salary, average salary, and earnings. The lower the percent female in an occupation, the higher the average salary is (but note the tipping point for starting salary is around 70% female).

The Success Gap

Table 5.3B includes all male seekers of female jobs and compares those who successfully found female jobs with those who were redirected into other locations. The wage differential by percent female in an occupation is again reflected here. Among those males who sought a job in a high-percent female occupation, the successful seekers are penalized monetarily. On average, they earn about 63% of what redirected male seekers do ($15,173 vs. $24,105). Note that where the redirected seekers relocate is also significant. Those who are in male jobs make considerably more than other redirected males. Economic incentives continue to be predictably structured by sex composition.

Men and Money in Female Jobs. Table 5.3C compares two kinds of male workers in female jobs: (a) premeditated finders who actually preferred a female job and (b) the diverted finders who did not state a preference or were looking somewhere else. There is little difference in their earnings ($15,173 and $15,880). This could be misleading since all of the 13 premeditated finders are white, but 27% of the diverted finders are minority (we are missing income data on one minority man). There is an earnings difference among whites of more than $2,000 ($15,173 vs. $17,298), but much of this difference can be attributed to older diverted finders who also have more experience and longer tenure; again we are reminded that it is a fallacy to assume that men in female jobs are a homogeneous group. Minority men are economically disadvantaged at $11,893, 31% below that of white men.[5]

Table 5.3A Actual Earnings for Male Workers in Three Categories of Female Majority Occupations; Starting Salary and Average Salary for Job

Percent Female in Occupation	Actual Earnings	Starting Salary for Job	Average Salary for Job
90-100 (n = 19)	$18,212	$13,258	$15,769
70-90 (n = 79)	$16,098	$13,133	$17,280
50-70 (n = 108)	$23,052	$17,232	$20,760

Table 5.3B Actual Earnings for Male Successful Seekers and Male Redirected Seekers of Female Occupations (75%-100% Female); Starting Salary and Average Salary for Job

	Actual Earnings	Starting Salary for Job	Average Salary for Job
Successful Seekers (N = 13)	$15,173	$13,066	$16,393
Redirected Seekers (N = 13)	$24,105*	$20,017	$22,800
By % Female in Current Job			
50-75 (n = 5)	$20,100	$15,748	$17,682
25-50 (n = 4)	$25,538	$26,030	$24,097
0-25 (n = 4)	$31,250	$19,515	$27,900

NOTE: *Data are missing on two respondents, both relocated in male jobs; n for total earnings is 11, for 0-25 category is 2.

Table 5.3C Actual Earnings for Male Premeditated Finders and Male Diverted Finders in Female Occupations (75%-100% Female), by Race; Starting Salary and Average Salary for Job

	Actual Earnings	Starting Salary for Job	Average Salary for Job
Premeditated Finders (N = 13, all white)	$15,173	$13,066	$16,393
Diverted Finders			
All (N = 61)	$15,880	$12,919	$16,325
White (N = 45)	$17,298	$13,744	$16,829
Nonwhite (N = 16)	$11,893	$10,736	$14,993

The Leaver Dilemma

In inquiring about the advantages or disadvantages of men's mobility through female occupations and into other jobs, we compare average salaries and actual earnings for the leavers—men who at one time held a job in the 75%-100% female range—with men who have different mobility patterns. Table 5.3D displays the results.

Part 1 of Table 5.3D compares male leavers with men who have not previously held a female-dominated job ("other males"). When we look at all men in those two categories, male leavers appear to be economically disadvantaged both in the types of jobs they find (indicated by lower starting salary and average salary for that position) and in the amount of their actual earnings (leavers $22,803, other males, $25,303).

A pattern becomes apparent, though, when we examine the two groups in the context of percent-female in their current job. If men who leave female occupations find work in any mixed-gender jobs (25%-75% female), they are disadvantaged economically. The jobs they find have both lower starting salaries and average salaries, and they earn about 15% less than all other men in that job type. For example, men who have left a female-dominated job and who find work in jobs 25%-50% female earn on average $20,463; men who are currently employed in the same percent female category, but who do not have experience in a female-dominated occupation, average $24,080—17% more. Different results occur for male leavers of female jobs who get jobs in male (0%-25% female) occupations. They earn, on average, $27,008— about 5% more than non-leaver males in male jobs ($25,889)—even though the leavers are in jobs with lower average pay (they earn above average for those jobs). Thus, for male leavers, a critical determinant of earnings is where they relocate.

To examine mobility patterns more closely, we look at men with other work experiences in Part 2 of Table 5.3D. First, we list figures for all males who are currently in a female occupation (stayers). As one would predict from our knowledge that female-dominated jobs pay less, male leavers (displayed in Part 1) earn significantly more ($22,803) than male stayers ($15,756), regardless of where leavers find current jobs.

Finally, we display a category of male consistents—men who have always been and are now located in a male-dominated occupation. There appears to be little earnings difference between men who have left female jobs but are now located in male jobs ($27,008) and male consistents ($26,893). However, the leavers seem to have arrived on a

Table 5.3D Actual Earnings for Male Leavers of Female Occupations, All Other Males, Male Stayers in Female Occupations, and Male Consistents in Male Occupations; Starting Salary and Average Salary for Jobs

Current Location: Means for All and by Percent Female in Current Job	Actual Earnings		Starting Salary for Job		Average Salary for Job	
	Male Leavers[1]	Other Males[2]	Male Leavers	Other Males	Male Leavers	Other Males
All	$22,803 (N = 105)	$25,303 (N = 1,224)	$18,016	$19,484	$20,971	$23,002
50%-75% Female	$19,866 (N = 27)	$23,038 (N = 96)	$16,007	$16,803	$18,760	$20,914
25%-50% Female	$20,463 (N = 38)	$24,080 (N = 245)	$17,076	$18,546	$20,336	$21,758
0%-25% Female	$27,008 (N = 40)	$25,889 (N = 883)	$20,103	$20,030	$22,905	$23,572

Male Workers With Other Types of Mobility Experience	Actual Earnings	Starting Salary for Job	Average Salary for Job
Male Stayers, Female Occupations[3] (N = 74)	$15,756	$12,945	$16,337
Male Consistents, Male Occupations[4] (N = 493)	$26,893	$20,251	$23,924

NOTE: [1]Males who have at one time held a job in a female-dominated occupation, but currently do not. Data are displayed for all workers in this category and also by percent-female in current location.
[2]Males who have not previously held a female-dominated job.
[3]All males who are currently in a female-dominated occupation (75%-100% female).
[4]Males who have always been and are now located in a male-dominated occupation (0%-25% female).

83

fast track—they are younger than consistents (37 vs. 40), average fewer years of experience (18 vs. 20), but exhibit longer tenure with their firm (13 years vs. 8). Apparently, they accrue an advantage via female-dominated occupations that allows them to accelerate into successful positions, where they also stay longer than men who have always been in male-dominated jobs.

We can conclude that three specific groups of males earn more than others: (a) men who aspire to and perceive opportunity in female occupations, but actually locate in male jobs (for redirected seekers, see Table 5.3B); (b) men who choose to gain experience (often supervisory) in female jobs and then relocate in male jobs (leavers in male jobs, Table 5.3D); and (c) men who gain experience in male jobs and stay in predominantly male occupations (male consistents, Table 5.3D). These findings clearly illustrate the import of including goal context and of precisely identifying gendered mobility tracks when we make assumptions about advantage and disadvantage via experience in sex-atypical occupations.

Table 5.4 further clarifies the impact of men's job mobility via female occupations on the salaries of the positions they hold and on their actual earnings. In comparing men who gain experience in female jobs and then relocate in male jobs (female job to male job) with those who have had consistently male jobs (suppressed category), we find a positive but insignificant difference in the positions they find (indicated by starting salary and average salary) and in earnings. After control variables, education, experience, and supervisory status are introduced, the coefficients are even smaller, and in the case of average salary are reversed. All remain insignificant at the .01 level. As indicated in Table 5.3D, men who gain experience via female occupations and then relocate in male jobs find an alternate mobility route that gains an advantage for them equal to those who have consistently remained in male-dominated jobs.

Men who were in female jobs but relocated in mixed jobs (25%-75% female) are significantly penalized in the jobs they find (starting and average salary) and in their actual earnings, even after controlling for education, experience, and supervisory position. They also earn significantly less than the salary reported as average for their job. Also, as expected, men who have been consistently in female jobs, as compared to men in consistently male jobs, are strongly disadvantaged.

Table 5.4 Results of Multiple Regression: Impact of Men's Job Mobility on Earnings, Starting Salary, and Average Salary,[a] Before and Net of Education, Experience, and Supervisory Status

	Impact on Log of Earnings Unstandardized Regression Coefficient			Impact on Log of Starting Salary Unstandardized Regression Coefficient			Impact on Log of Average Salary Unstandardized Regression Coefficient		
Mobility Pattern	No Controls	Net of Educ.	Net of Educ., Exper., Supervise	No Controls	Net of Educ.	Net of Educ., Exper., Supervise	No Controls	Net of Educ.	Net of Educ., Exper., Supervise
Female Job to Male Job	.14	.06	.01	.04	.02	.00	.01	-.02	-.03
Female Job to Mixed Job	-.29*	-.31*	-.30*	-.14*	-.15*	-.15*	-.15*	-.17*	-.16*
Consistently Female Job	-.73*	-.66*	-.62*	-.40*	-.39*	-.37*	-.35*	-.33*	-.32*

NOTE: [a]Each dependent variable (earnings, starting salary, and average salary) is logged, then regressed on dummy variables representing mobility patterns, both before and after control variables are introduced. Not all mobility category coefficients are reported. The comparison group (suppressed category) is consistently male job, that is, those who have either always had a high-percent male job or have moved from one male job to another.

*p < .01

85

Summary and Conclusion

Previous research has shown how social control mechanisms contribute to sex segregation of occupations both through individual decisions that preclude many men from seeking employment in female-dominated jobs and through structural opportunities that propel men into more "male-defined" areas. There are cultural sanctions that keep men out of women's work, and incentives that advantage men over women, even in female occupations. We expand our understanding of gender stratification by refining our knowledge of how and whether men accrue advantage via female occupations. Three issues are important for providing a framework for research in occupational inequality: (a) distinctions between individual-level social control, which operates normatively both directly and through group mediation, and structural social control, which is also often founded on gender expectations, and emerges in various forms of constraints and incentives; (b) contextual considerations of goals and aspirations; and (c) processual tracking of mobility patterns in and out of occupations defined by percent female in them.

In clarifying individual-level social control, we not only recognize mechanisms that restrict individual men from entering female-dominated occupations, but we also consider group-mediated sanctions that offer a more complete explanation for the small percentage of men who seek work in jobs where women are a majority. An extremely small number—only 5.5% of the males in our sample—said they preferred a job that is high-percent female. It is theoretically important to conceptualize how status maintenance and group ideology work to uphold male dominance. Social control through group mediation offers a way to understand how hegemonic masculinity is supported, despite individual desires and interests. Most men understand what kind of work "real men" do. On the other hand, alternative masculinity definitions may be influenced through an interplay between structural factors and the culturally defined salience of race/ethnicity and sexual orientation.

Further, there are constraints beyond those that deter men from seeking women's work. Only 50% of men in our sample who wanted and sought female jobs actually got them. Previous theories have not actively dealt with the fact that many men are actually blocked from entering female-dominated occupations. At the individual level, employers may use both personal gender prejudice and also more generalized gendered expectations to arrive at decisions that turn men away. We have evidence that some men seem to genuinely desire and seek the kind of work that certain female occupations offer, such as caring for and teaching young children. But many are denied access—some are blocked even when they are trained for a specific occupation, such as we witnessed with elementary school teachers.

In addition, structural-level barriers deter certain groups from employment in female jobs. Recalling that unsuccessful seekers of male jobs were not characteristically different from those who did find male jobs, female-typed jobs are more selective, at least for men. Apparently, successful male seekers of female jobs must typically be young, unencumbered with family responsibilities, and more willing to work part-time and at unprotected jobs in small firms—both able and willing to take risks. Nonetheless, the "glass escalator" effect found by Williams often carries them into more prestigious and better-paying jobs; more than half of those who wanted female jobs and didn't get them were placed in management. However, those men did state that they strongly preferred other positions.

We emphasize the context of goals in order to build a general gender model that more precisely handles both women's and men's crossing over into jobs defined as gender-traditional. Not only does this inclusion allow us to consider how men and women have different purposes and incentives, but it also encompasses status and power differentials among men. We can no longer assume that men in female jobs, though numerically few, are a homogeneous group relative to goals, aspirations, positions, and expectations. For example, when we differentiate between men who actively sought jobs in female-dominated occupations and those who fell through the trapdoor, it becomes evident that some men seem to "settle" for these jobs, while others seem to use them as a rung in a career ladder. Furthermore, for a select few, it works. Those who successfully use this channel also gain financial advantage.

Goals also reflect changes in aspirations relative to perceived opportunity, which may be different for men and women. Some men, who may rely on hegemonic masculinity in a way that women cannot, seem to perceive and find a diversity of alternate routes to success. Data in this study identify three groups of men who have accrued economic advantage from gender segregation: men who aspire to female jobs but are escalated into better, more male-defined positions; men who gain experience and supervisory status in female jobs, then move into male jobs; and men who gain experience in male jobs and stay in predominantly male-defined occupations. Additionally, groups of men who are typically denied resources may construct different responses based on availability and opportunity.

A simpler segregation model might assume that male advantage in female jobs results only from overtly discriminatory practices by employers. And certainly we can document that kind of discrimination. For example, a male bookkeeper who has even limited experience may meet expectations (including gender stereotypes) as a "leader," while also being attractively cost-efficient to the organization, and thus be hired as a financial manager. However, as we demonstrate, those who successfully locate in female jobs have very specific characteristics: young, well-educated men with few if any family responsibilities. Because they are seeking jobs in female occupations where pay is historically and consistently low, they must be somehow motivated to move into an area that may yield potential, but also must be better able to afford a risk or delay in financial rewards. Further, not all men in female occupations accrue an advantage. In fact, while in female occupations, they earn less than other males, and they remain economically disadvantaged unless they are able to relocate in a high-percent male job. Many talented gay men, for example, are working at positions far beneath their qualifications and capabilities because of discrimination (Levine, 1992).

Thus inequities that are initially attributed to simple sex discrimination are actually a more complex web of relations that affect specific groups of both men and women. It is well-known that women are disadvantaged by sex segregation and discriminatory practices in the labor market. This study suggests that while most men carry their gender advantage with them, at least some men who attempt to cross over into female-dominated occupations are blocked—and perhaps there are even greater numbers, which we could not isolate with these data, who might have preferred traditionally female jobs but never even considered them. Organizations do seem to be important sites of a process by which advantage and disadvantage is patterned and organized, based on distinctions between male and female, masculinity and femininity. Only when we understand gender as a form of oppression, which not only works by providing gendered cognitive maps via social control for individuals, but which is also maintained and "constantly constituted" (Connell, 1987) in daily organizational practices, do we see how gender systematically works to disadvantage people. While we hesitate to draw strong conclusions from these data, given the limited number of men who seek and find jobs in female-dominated occupations, the patterns we do identify clearly suggest that a more thorough investigation of the nature of how organizations become gendered should prove fruitful. We should further consider how hegemonic masculinity is used in organizations, regardless of sex composition, to define eligibility, leadership, and privilege of all individuals not meeting the ideals of masculinity.

Notes

1. This research was supported by a grant to Wayne J. Villemez and William P. Bridges from the National Science Foundation (SES-8012117).
2. Elsewhere we present corollary data on females that reveal a very similar pattern.
3. While this division results in very small Ns, we believe the comparison is theoretically important. The subsample is from a very large random sample, and the data fall into very clear patterns; we have no reason to suspect that our small subsample is in any way atypical. A man actively seeking traditionally female employment is a rare event, and our sample percentage simply reflects this fact.
4. For brevity, we use the term *minority* to refer to both black and Hispanic males. In this instance, 11 respondents are black, 6 are Hispanic.
5. Again, these data strongly suggest that all three concepts—social control, goals, and mobility opportunities—may differ dramatically by race.

References

Acker, J. (1990). Hierarchies, jobs, bodies: A theory of gendered organizations. *Gender & Society, 4*, 139-158.
Cazenave, N. A. (1984). Race, socioeconomic status, and age: The social context of American masculinity. *Sex Roles, 11*, 639-656.
Connell, R. W. (1987). *Gender and power: Society, the person and sexual politics*. Palo Alto, CA: Stanford University Press.
Connell, R. W. (1990). A whole new world: Remaking masculinity in the context of the environmental movement. *Gender & Society, 4*, 452-478.
England, P., Farkas, G., Kilbourne, B., & Dou, T. (1988). Estimating the wage consequences of sex segregation: A fixed effects model. *American Sociological Review, 53*, 544-588.
Hall, E. J. (1993). Waitering/waitressing: Engendering the work of table servers. *Gender & Society*.
Jacobs, J. A. (1989). *Revolving doors: Sex segregation and women's careers*. Palo Alto, CA: Stanford University Press.
Leidner, R. (1991). Serving hamburgers and selling insurance: Gender, work, and identity in interactive service jobs. *Gender & Society, 5*, 154-177.
Levine, M. P. (1992). The status of gay men in the workplace. In M. S. Kimmel & M. A. Messner (Eds.), *Men's lives* (pp. 251-266). New York: Macmillan.
Majors, R. (1992). Cool pose: The proud signature of black survival. In M. S. Kimmel & M. A. Messner (Eds.), *Men's lives* (pp. 131-134). New York: Macmillan.

Messner, M. (1992). Boyhood, organized sports, and the construction of masculinity. In M. S. Kimmel & M. A. Messner (Eds.), *Men's lives* (pp. 161-175). New York: Macmillan.

Morrison, A. M., White, R. P., Van Velsor, E., & The Center for Creative Leadership. (1987). *Breaking the glass ceiling: Can women reach the top of America's largest corporations?*. Reading, MA: Addison-Wesley.

Reskin, B. F. (1988). Bringing the men back in: Sex differentiation and the devaluation of women's work. *Gender & Society, 2*, 58-81.

Reskin, B. F., & Roos, P. A. (1990). *Job queues, gender queues: Explaining women's inroads into male occupations.* Philadelphia: Temple University Press.

Stromberg, A. H., & Harkess, S. (Eds.). (1988). *Women working: Theories and facts in perspective* (2nd ed.). Mountain View, CA: Mayfield.

Villemez, W. J., Williams, L. S., Bridges, W. P., & Morris, J. (1992). *Market, choice, or constraint? Occupational sex segregation and outcomes.* Unpublished manuscript.

Williams, C. L. (1989). *Gender differences at work: Women and men in nontraditional occupations.* Berkeley: University of California Press.

Williams, C. L. (1992). The glass escalator: Hidden advantages for men in the "female" professions. *Social Problems, 39*, 253-267.

Zinn, M. B. (1992). Chicano men and masculinity. In M. S. Kimmel & M. A. Messner (Eds.), *Men's lives* (pp. 67-76). New York: Macmillan.

6
Men in Female-Dominated Occupations

A Cross-Cultural Comparison

KAISA KAUPPINEN-TOROPAINEN
JOHANNA LAMMI

This chapter gives a cross-cultural overview of men's experiences in gender-atypical occupations. The studies mainly concern men employed in nursing and other caregiving occupations in the Nordic countries. Some references are made to research in the United States and Great Britain. According to the literature, there is very little empirical research that consciously focuses on the position of men in female occupations in Germany and France. Thus the cross-cultural view is based mainly on men's experiences in the Nordic countries. Even in these countries, the research is restricted and practical-oriented; it is usually published in the native languages as research reports or working papers, or it is in the form of documents prepared by the Equality Office Personnel. The chapter also presents the results of an empirical study of male kindergarten and primary school teachers and practical nurses in the Nordic countries (Finland, Norway, Sweden) and the United States. The focus of the study is on the nontraditional men's subjective perceptions of cross-gender interaction (collegiality, friendship, envy) at work.

Gender-Segregated Labor Market

It is typical for modern Western societies that the labor market is sharply segregated by gender; there are distinct men's and women's occupations, workplaces, and work tasks. As a result of this segregation, many jobs are labeled as male- or female-appropriate. The division of labor is reminiscent of preindustrial society, where men took care of the material production while women provided domestic care and nurturance (Österberg & Hedman, 1989). There is no indication that the segregation at work will greatly diminish in the near future. In the United States, for example, in 1900 as well as in 1970, more than half of all employed women worked in occupations where more than 70% of the workers were women (Fottler, 1976).

Similarly, throughout the Nordic countries (Denmark, Finland, Norway, and Sweden), there is a sharp distinction between what is women's and what is men's work (Haavio-Mannila & Kauppinen, 1992). In Finland, Norway, and Sweden every other man has a distinctly male-dominated job, where the percentage of women is at the most 10; in Denmark 39% of occupationally active men work in jobs entirely dominated by men (Table 6.1). In the United States, in 1980 as many as two-thirds of all employed men worked in professions that were 80% male (Williams, 1989).

The Danish labor market is slightly less segregated by gender than those of the other Nordic countries. This is mostly due to the relatively high proportion of women (35%) working either in balanced or male-dominated occupations. In the other Nordic countries, this proportion is considerably lower: in Finland 25%, in Sweden 21%, and in Norway 15%. At the most, about 10% of all employed people work in occupations that have a balanced ratio of men and women. As a result of this segregation, only a small proportion of both men and women (1%-3%) in each Nordic country work in occupations where they represent the minority gender.

Men and women each work within their clearly defined spheres of the labor market. The women's sphere is characterized by an emphasis on providing services or taking care of people, while looking after the material world is largely regarded as a typical man's job.

In 1990, the top 10 occupations of men in Finland were (*Women and Men in Finland,* 1991): building worker; technician; plumber, mason, welder; driver of motor vehicles; toolmaker, fitter-assembler, machine repairman; electrician, electronic worker, and telephone assembler; executive of business enterprises and organizations; shop assistant and

Table 6.1 The Employed Population According to Gender in the Nordic Countries, in Percent

Men's Share in the Occupation	Finland 1986		Sweden 1980		Norway 1986		Denmark 1981	
	Men	Women	Men	Women	Men	Women	Men	Women
0%-10%	2	49	1	29	3	53	1	29
10%-40%	8	26	13	50	11	32	7	36
40%-60%	10	10	6	7	6	6	10	15
60%-90%	35	13	33	11	30	8	43	18
90%-100%	45	2	47	3	50	1	39	2
Total, %	100	100	100	100	100	100	100	100
(1000)	1,264	1,167	2,208	1,804	891	787	1,485	1,140

SOURCE: *Kvinnor och män i Norden* [Women and Men in the Nordic Countries], 1988.
NOTE: (1,000) = the number of men and women in each country is given x 1,000. For example: Finland = 1,264 x 1,000 for men; 1,167 x 1,000 for women.

foreman; sales representative, office salesman; agricultural and forestry worker. The top 10 occupations of women, in which the men represent the minority gender, were (*Women and Men in Finland,* 1991): secretary, typist, general office worker; shop assistant and shop supervisor; cleaner, hospital assistant; registered nurse, practical nurse, laboratory and dental assistant; chef and cook, kitchen hand, restaurant worker; teacher; bank and insurance employee; social worker and day-care worker; home assistant, home helper and private family day-care worker; financial planner, accountancy personnel.

Even though gender segregation in working life is considerable, men and women, nevertheless, have numerous professional contacts with each other. The daily contacts are less intensively segregated according to gender than are the work tasks performed by men and women (Kauppinen-Toropainen, Haavio-Mannila, & Kandolin, 1984). A Finnish case study on work contacts by Haavio-Mannila (1990) showed that 60% of the men and 72% of the women were in daily professional contact with the opposite gender. Only 7% of the men and 5% of the women hardly met people of the opposite gender during the working day. The numerous contacts between men and women at work expose them to formal as well as informal cross-gender interaction (Haavio-Mannila, Kauppinen-Toropainen, & Kandolin, 1988). It may also disguise the fact that the work tasks performed by women and men are usually different.

Men Are Less Active Than Women
in Crossing the Gender Barrier

Men have been less active than women in crossing the occupational gender barrier. One reason is that women get more material benefits from doing so. Our Finnish study, based on a representative sample of the entire wage-earning population in Finland (Kauppinen-Toropainen, Haavio-Mannila, & Kandolin, 1989), showed that women profited from the fact that they performed the same sort of work as men: The salaries of these women were higher and their work was more autonomous, more challenging, and less rigidly controlled than that of the women who performed work that was typically done by women.

For men, the effects of working in nontraditional work roles were the opposite from those for women (Kauppinen-Toropainen et al., 1989). The work performed by the nontraditional men was less autonomous and more routinized, and the rhythm of work was more rigidly controlled than the work performed by men in status-comparable male occupations. A consistent result also was that men's salaries were significantly lower in situations where they performed the same sort of work as women, when compared to the salaries of men in typical male occupations. However, the nontraditional men's salaries were considerably higher than their female colleagues' salaries.

The reason for the nontraditional men's higher salaries in relation to their female peers' salaries was that the men more frequently held supervisory and administrative positions. Also, men specialized in more innovative and special work roles, for example, specialist teacher, emergency room nurse, project leader for boys in day-care centers, where the salaries were more freely influenced by individual competence and performance. Women, on the other hand, held "ordinary" female jobs, in which salaries were more strictly based on a collective-bargaining system with little or no room for individual negotiation.

The salary difference can partly be due to the differences in men's and women's working hours. A study of male and female nurses in Sweden revealed that the men's average working hours in hospitals and healthcare centers were considerably longer than those of their female co-workers; half of the women had a part-time job, whereas only 13% of the men worked on a part-time arrangement (Rosby-Björkquist & Knutsson, 1986). Men's longer working hours were also documented in a study of male and female nurses in Norway (Sandnes & Tanem, 1991). Even though men's working hours in female occupations are usually longer than those of their female peers, the average working hours for men in female jobs are significantly shorter than for men in general (Hayes, 1989).

Even though men often are advantaged in relation to their female peers in typical female jobs, very few men have actually crossed the occupational gender barrier. In fact fewer men today than some 20 years ago work as social workers in Finland, while growing numbers of young women are entering such typically male-dominated fields as medicine, law, veterinary science, and optometry (Kauppinen-Toropainen, 1991b; Riska & Wegar, 1989; Silius, 1992). Likewise, in Sweden, the proportion of male psychiatric nurses had fallen, not increased, between 1960 and 1985. And in the United States, in 1990, there were fewer men in primary school teaching than in 1980 (Table 6.2).

Since the early 1970s, training as kindergarten teachers has been made available for men in Finland. And in 1955 the first man graduated from a nursing school in Sweden, and 10 years later in Finland (Lammi, 1992). Nevertheless, the proportion of men among the practical nurses and kindergarten teachers has remained very small throughout the Nordic countries, which is also the case in the United States, where a mere 4% of the child-care workers were men in 1991 (Table 6.2). In 1980 less than 3% of all registered nurses in the United States were men (Williams, 1989). There has been no rush among men to enter typically female professions.

The proportion of men among the psychiatric nurses has traditionally been greater than in any other area of nursing; about one-third of the psychiatric nurses are men in each Nordic country (Table 6.2). Psychiatric nursing has been regarded as more masculine and better suited for men, since the work demands physical strength and special skills to handle difficult and potentially aggressive patients (Brown & Stones, 1973; Sandnes & Tanem, 1991; Williams, 1989).

Our study of psychiatric nurses in Finland proved that the men more often than the women worked with difficult and aggressive patients (Kauppinen-Toropainen, 1991c). The men also had less feelings of sympathy toward their patients, and they reported significantly more symptoms of burnout and stress than their women colleagues. Sandnes & Tanem (1991) reported similar results in Norway. These differences may reflect differences in the men's and women's working positions in mental hospitals, for example, men tend to work with more severely disturbed patients than women, and this is known to cause burnout and stress (Maslach & Jackson, 1986). The differences may also reflect differences in men's and women's professional strategies and orientations toward sick people; the men more often than the women felt that working intensively with patients caused them psychological stress. The women's socialization process may sensitize them better for their professional caregiver roles. The reason may also be that it is more difficult for women, due to this socialization process, to confess burnout symptoms (Barnett, Bienir, & Baruch, 1987; Freudenberger & North, 1985).

The Male Mode of Specialization:
Male Bastions Within Female Occupations

For years, nursing has been one of the dream jobs of young women in Finland, as elsewhere. "Calling" has been emphasized as one important aspect of the work (Lammi, 1992). A study of nursing students in

Table 6.2 Men's Share in Female Occupations, in Percent

	1960	1970	1975	1980	1985	1991
Registered nurse						
Finland	0	0.8	2.0	2.2	2.4	—
Sweden	0	0.8	3.4	6.1	6.1	—
United States	—	2.7	—	4.1	—	5.0
Psychiatric nurse						
Finland	—	29.3	29.5	31.9	35.1	—
Sweden	43.1	36.8	37.1	34.8	32.8	—
Kindergarten teacher						
Finland	0	0.2	1.0	3.8	4.5	—
Sweden	0	0.5	3.8	5.5	8.1	—
Norway	—	0.1	—	5.0	—	—
United States						
Child-care worker						
United States	—	7.5	—	6.8	—	4.0
Primary teacher						
United States	—	16.1	—	24.6	—	14.0

Source for the Nordic Data: Lammi, 1992.
Source for the U.S. Data: Taeuber & Valdisera, 1986; Bureau of Labor Statistics, U.S. Dept. of Labor, 1992.

England showed that while the female students typically said that nursing had been their dream since early adolescence, the male students said that they had been uncertain about their career and had decided to go to nursing school by mere chance, often after experiencing unemployment in the labor market (Brown & Stones, 1973). For these men, nursing was not a calling or a dream job, it was just a job among many others. An important aspect for the male students was that a job in nursing provided them with an economically secure career in times of economic uncertainty.

Economic security was also mentioned by male nurses in Sweden as a central reason for enroling in nursing school (Carlsson & Bergknut, 1988). The study, which covered 354 male nurses, brought out many common features; 57% had specialized in psychiatric nursing, 50% were trade union activists, and one-third held an administrative or teaching job. And 40% said that they would not choose nursing as a career again, the main reason being the low salary and hard work.

A study of male auxiliary nurses in Norway (Sandnes & Tanem, 1991) showed that the men specialized in work roles in which the need for direct interaction with the patients was minimal: The men typically specialized in anaesthesia, emergency room, or intensive care nursing, where they worked primarily as experts on technical machinery, not as caregivers as such. Very seldom did the male nurses have work roles where their patients were either young children or adolescents, who need constant attention and more personalized care. Similarly, an interview study of men working in "people jobs" in Finland showed that the men very seldom had elderly or handicapped people as their customers. This kind of intensive "people work" was defined as proper female work (Kauppinen-Toropainen, 1991b).

Also Rosby-Björkquist and Knutsson (1986) reported in their study of Swedish male and female nurses that the male nurses were more inclined to be involved with research and technical equipment, whereas the women were more satisfied with their work when it was normal patient care. Williams (1989) noted in her study of male nurses in the United States that the rare men in the field preserved their masculine working style and created a special male bastion; the men specialized in intensive care, emergency care, or administration.

The studies in Finland, Sweden, and Norway (Haavio-Mannila, 1989; Lammi, 1992; Rosby-Björquist & Knutsson, 1986; Sandnes & Tanem, 1991; Sverdrup Berg, 1980) unanimously demonstrate that the few men who work in healthcare occupations are encouraged by their female colleagues to participate in trade unions and other professional activities. Consequently, men tend to be overrepresented in trade unions as elected representatives and functionaries. For the men, the role of an elected trade union activist presents another opportunity to pursue a "masculine" career in a woman-dominated occupation. This, in turn, contributes to the men's special position at work—the trade union activity brings men professional as well as personal clout and esteem.

The results show that, within the healthcare sector, the few, or solo, men have an opportunity to specialize in fields that support their masculine identity; the men actively shape their work role to be more task-oriented and less people-oriented. In doing so, the men tend to distance themselves from their female colleagues and the feminine working strategy, which stresses care-oriented rationality. The men strive to redefine their professional activity to suit the masculine gender (Gilligan, 1982; Gilligan & Pollak, 1988; Ve, 1992).

It seems to be a universal phenomenon that men in female professions hold special male-appropriate positions. This came out in our study in Moscow where we, together with our Russian colleagues, conducted a study of men and women in the medical profession (Kauppinen-Toropainen, 1991a). Unlike in most Western countries (Walsh, 1977), medicine in the former Soviet Union has been a typical female profession; 87% of the medical doctors were women in the Soviet Union in 1985 (Lapidus, 1988). We found that the male doctors enjoyed significantly higher salaries (the women's salaries were 25% lower than those of the men) and held more prominent positions in the hospital hierarchy than their women colleagues. Also, there was a clear distinction between the men's and women's specialization areas: While the women's specialty fields typically were basic medicine, gynecology, and pediatrics, the men's specialty fields were surgery, research, and psychiatry. Since the women doctors more often than the men complained about stress and felt that their capacity to cope with stressful situations was deteriorating, our conclusion was that it is more burdensome for professional women than for men to manage both family and professional issues in times of political and social change (Kauppinen-Toropainen, 1991a).

Men's Adaptation to the Feminine Work Environment

A male nurse or a kindergarten teacher is a token, a solo member of his gender in a predominantly female-dominated field (Kanter, 1977).

Due to this solo position, the man attracts special positive attention, which, according to many studies, brings him more respect and autonomy relative to his female co-workers (Epstein, 1970, 1988; Kanter, 1977; Kauppinen-Toropainen, 1987).

The research shows that the nontraditional men usually receive encouragement and support from their female colleagues (Kauppinen-Toropainen, 1992; Lammi, 1992; Lindgren, 1983; Wharton & Baron, 1987; Williams, 1989). Women tend to welcome men into female occupations because they believe that an increase in the number of men in the profession can enhance the status, prestige, and, they hope, the pay of the profession. These supportive attitudes help men's adaptation into the feminine workplace culture. Nevertheless, some women feel angry and frustrated because of the advantage and special treatment the men usually have over the female workers in their promotions and careers.

Our Finnish study of male psychiatric nurses and waiters (Haavio-Mannila, Kauppinen-Toropainen, & Kandolin, 1991) showed that the nurses and the waiters experienced the attitudes of their female co-workers as supportive, friendly, and equal. When we compared these attitudes to the attitudes expressed by the police officers and technicians included in our sample as representatives of typical male professions, we found that the police officers and technicians experienced co-workers' attitudes as significantly less supportive and less friendly. The male workplace culture was much more competitive and aggressive than the female one. We posed the same set of questions to the male nurses surveyed in the United States. The American nurses' answers mirrored those of their Finnish counterparts: Of the 57 American nurses, one-quarter said the attitudes were supportive, 28% felt the attitudes to be equal, and 40% said the attitudes were friendly.

The differences found in the co-worker attitudes between the female versus male professions may reflect differences in the workplace culture because the masculine culture is less cooperative than the female one. The differences may also reflect the positive special treatment that the solo men in female-dominated occupations usually receive.

The research, however, shows that the men's psychological adaptation into female-dominated working places does not happen without difficulties. According to the Swedish male nurses surveyed by Carlsson & Bergknut (1988), the men did not find the feminine workplace culture very easy to cope with, and they felt like outsiders. The men's typical notion was that their presence normalized the feminine workplace atmosphere; the men felt there was less conflict and gossiping. The

Norwegian male auxiliary nurses surveyed by Sandnes and Tanem (1991) shared this notion.

We came to the same conclusion when interviewing the male kindergarten teachers in Finland: The men often felt they "cheered up" the feminine workplace atmosphere by bringing new challenges, viewpoints, and ideas (Kauppinen-Toropainen, 1992). The men referred to the same phenomenon as their Swedish and Norwegian counterparts; that is, they felt that their presence normalized the female workplace atmosphere. The men also complained that it was abnormal to have workplaces exclusively dominated by one gender, especially when the work dealt with young children. The men said that there should be both men and women in the day care centers, just as there are men and women in the real world. Many men found it difficult to fully integrate into female-dominated work teams and they missed male companionship.

Similarly, for the Swedish practical nurses surveyed by Erngren, Birath, and Linberg (1986), the interaction with women often caused problems and they had seriously thought about changing jobs. Other reasons for wishing to change jobs were poor salary, difficulties in career development, and the low status of the work. Robinson (1979) noted, in his follow-up study of kindergarten teachers in the United States, that the men had changed jobs more often than the women within the 2-year follow-up period; the men did not find the female-dominated work settings rewarding enough.

Kadushin (1976) has argued that, for men, other men and their attitudes are more important, as a frame of reference in defining men's sense of satisfaction with work, than their women colleagues' attitudes. In this comparison, the nontraditional men often see themselves as failures; their jobs are less appreciated, their salaries are lower, and their occupational choice is more often questioned. In Kadushin's study, the other men regarded the male social workers as impractical idealists.

Similarly, in a study of 273 male kindergarten teachers in Norway (Sverdrup Berg, 1980), 40% of the men reported problems in interacting with other men, as a result of their working in a female-labeled profession; they felt that the other men did not take them seriously. The men also experienced constant pressure from their female colleagues to initiate athletic sports games with the children and act as male role models for the children. The women did not entrust the care of small children to men; it was considered a proper female job.

We found the same phenomenon when conducting interviews with the male kindergarten teachers in Finland. The men felt they were trapped in a double-bind situation: They were seen as strangers by other men, while their women colleagues pushed them into stereotyped masculine roles. Women expected them to assume a traditional masculine role (change the light bulb, be a chauffeur, initiate action-type play with boys) and resisted the men's insistence to do "ordinary" day-care work with the children (Kauppinen-Toropainen, 1987). This is one version of the sex-role spillover, as described by Barbara Gutek: Men's sex-role spills over to their professional role (Gutek, 1985).

One strategy for some token men is that they seek a man's company at the workplace, be it a janitor, a driver, or any male person with whom they can discuss mutually interesting male topics, such as sports and cars (Williams, 1989). This can be seen as a symptom of men's homosocial tendencies, as described by Lipman-Blumen (1976). Homosocial tendencies mean that men are attracted to other men and enjoy each other's company. Williams (1989) noted, in her study of male nurses, that the men actively sought the company of male physicians with whom they could share work and nonwork interests. Partly due to this informal interaction and male companionship, the male doctors took the male nurses more seriously and treated them more professionally than the female nurses. The female nurses were more often targets of flirting, teasing, and verbal harassment by the physicians.

Cross-Gender Interaction:
Friendship, Collegiality, and Envy

We now turn to a cross-cultural comparison of male kindergarten and primary school teachers as well as practical nurses in the Nordic countries and the United States. The data for the study were collected with a mailed questionnaire in 1986 and 1988; only the Finnish kindergarten teachers were personally interviewed by the researchers in 1985 (Kauppinen-Toropainen, 1987). The idea was to find both similarities and dissimilarities in men's subjective experiences in gender-atypical professions. The main emphasis was on the quality of work and cross-gender interaction at work.

The respondents in each country were members of their respective professional unions, from which their names were obtained. The nurses in Finland were specialized nurses for the handicapped, of whom 8% were men in 1985 (Haavio-Mannila, 1989). In the other countries, the nurses were "ordinary" practical nurses registered in their respective unions. The kindergarten teachers in the Nordic countries work in municipally managed day-care centers, where the children's ages range between 1 and 6 years.

The immediate colleagues of most men, that is, the persons who performed the same sort of work as they did, were mostly or only women (Table 6.3). This strong female domination in the men's professional contacts was marked for the kindergarten teachers in the Nordic countries. The nurses' professional contacts were more mixed regarding their gender composition. This concerns particularly the Finnish nurses for the handicapped, of whom nearly half said that they had both men and women colleagues. This is a reflection of the nurses' and kindergarten teachers' different working environments. The teachers are more restricted in their work roles and contacts, whereas the nurses have more freedom to shape their professional activity according to their preferences. Also, the hospital settings are bigger and give more opportunity for specialization, while the kindergartens and day-care centers are smaller and more closed in this regard.

Only in the United States was there no difference between the primary school teachers and nurses regarding the gender composition of their professional contacts. The reason may be that the primary schools in the United States are more integral units of the school system—thus the male primary school teachers have a better opportunity to mix with the other male colleagues.

The men's informal friendship contacts were less strictly confined to women; many mentioned both men and women as their personal friends at work. The kindergarten teachers in Finland and Sweden, less often than the nurses, mentioned men as their personal friends among workmates. This may reflect that their opportunities for informal contacts beyond the immediate professional interaction are more restricted.

There was also an indication, most notably among the Danish nurses and the Swedish kindergarten teachers, that the men had no personal friends among their workmates. This may reflect the men's feeling of social isolation at a female-dominated workplace. One reason why the men seldom mentioned having personal friends at work may reflect their professional strategy: In order to maintain collegiality, the men refrain from too intimate and personal contacts with their female colleagues. This helps to ensure "erotic peace" at work, which is apt to prevent sexual rivalry (Haavio-Mannila et al., 1988; Liljeström, 1981).

Table 6.3 Cross-Gender Interaction at Work for the Male Kindergarten and Primary School Teachers and Practical Nurses

	Finland		Denmark		Sweden		United States	
	Kindergarten Teacher	Nurse for the Handicapped	Kindergarten Teacher	Registered Nurse	Kindergarten Teacher	Registered Nurse	Primary Teacher	Registered Nurse
Professional contacts (%)								
only women	63	10	24	8	44	11	0	9
mostly women	28	43	63	61	33	44	67	74
both men and women	0	45	10	26	14	24	29	16
only/mostly men	0	1	3	1	0	2	0	0
no colleagues	9 ***	1	0 *	0	0 ***	4	4 n.s.	1
total, %	100	100	100	100	100	100	100	100
number of respondents	32	74	59	89	43	54	52	57
Has personal friends among workmates (%)								
only women	43	5	15	22	23	9	2	14
only men	7	12	5	1	8	6	2	4
both men and women	20	62	51	33	23	60	83	63
no friends	30 ***	21	29 *	44	46 **	25	13 *	19
total, %	100	100	100	100	100	100	100	100
Has been an object of envy (%)	22 *	43	16	16	7 **	26	37 n.s.	30
Has a supportive mentor (%)	a)	20	52	74	69	80	87	86

"I enjoy my work" (%)

agrees completely	56	20	32	51	39	20	58	23
agrees to some extent	31	46	36	28	37	43	37	60
difficult to say	3	25	22	17	17	24	2	7
disagrees to some extent/ completely	10 **	8	10 n.s.	4	7 n.s.	13	3 **	10
total, %	100	100	100	100	100	100	100	100

"I find my work interesting and challenging" (%)

always	59	27	34	42	42	35	52	35
often	34	42	42	39	42	41	36	49
sometimes	6	22	24	17	14	17	12	16
never	0 **	8	0 n.s.	2	2 n.s.	7	0 n.s.	0
total, %	100	100	100	100	100	100	100	100

a) the question was not presented
n.s. = not significant, * = $p < 0.05$, ** = $p < 0.01$, *** = $p < 0.001$

The Finnish and Swedish nurses, more often than the kindergarten teachers, said that they had been objects of envy because of their success and achievement at work. The Danish nurses least experienced envious attitudes (Table 6.3). We could sense these tensions when interviewing the kindergarten teachers in Finland. The men often said that they were envied by their female colleagues because they were popular among the children and the parents, and because they were seen as father figures for many children, especially for those coming from single-parent families. The women kindergarten teachers often felt that the men's role was exaggerated. Also they felt that the men were treated as favorites by the children and the parents mostly because of their maleness and greater visibility—not because of their professional superiority. Thus the men's special position in female-dominated workplaces can lead to conflicts, envy, and frustrations. In this regard, the gender dimension in nursing is less sensitive.

The American nurses and teachers had a mentor more often than the others (Table 6.3). A mentor is a person who is in a superior position or otherwise influential in the field, and who is supportive and encouraging. An active mentor can provide the protégé with information about new job openings and advancement opportunities, and can help develop professional skills on the job (Epstein, 1988; Yoder, 1985). The nurses and teachers in the American workplaces could, in 87% of the cases, name a mentor who was supportive and encouraging. Their Danish and Swedish counterparts had the benefit of a supportive mentor far more often than their colleagues in the Finnish workplaces, where the mentoring system is less common. The mentor for the men was as often a man as a woman.

The availability of a mentor helps explain why men are often promoted to administrative and other special jobs in female professions. Men get promoted as headmasters and directors of primary schools or day-care centers, or they are encouraged to change jobs or continue their studies. The Finnish kindergarten teachers were very conscious of these attitudes, and they were also given information about new job opportunities and were encouraged to apply for them. Of the Swedish nurses surveyed by Erngren et al. (1986), half were contemplating a change in occupation, one possibility being a consultant for a pharmaceutical firm. In order to pursue a new career, one needs an experienced person or an active role model to encourage exploring new opportunities (Yoder, 1985). This kind of support partly explains why the men in female-dominated professions often occupy more innovative work roles: They are actively pushed into these positions.

It is not a surprise that the men usually found their work interesting and challenging (Table 6.3). In Finland and the United States, there was a slight tendency for the kindergarten and primary school teachers to experience their work as somewhat more interesting and challenging than did the nurses. This general positive attitude toward work translated into high work satisfaction, which was especially notable among the American and Finnish teachers; more than half of them completely agreed with the statement that they enjoyed their work very much. In this sense, the nontraditional men represent a privileged group of workers.

Summary and Conclusions

It is typical in modern Western societies for the labor market to be sharply segregated by gender. There are distinct men's and women's occupations, workplaces, and work tasks. The women's sphere is characterized by an emphasis on providing services and taking care of people, while looking after the material world is largely regarded as a typical man's job.

It is also a common phenomenon that men have been less active than women in crossing the occupational gender barrier. One reason is that the men get fewer material benefits than women from doing so. Also, the psychological barrier is still relatively high; men are afraid of the stigma of working in a feminine profession. This was evident in our Finnish study, which showed that for men, the effects of working in gender-atypical work roles were the opposite from those for women—the women's salaries were higher but the men's salaries were lower than the average men's salaries. The nontraditional men's salaries were, however, significantly higher than their female co-workers' salaries. Our conclusion was that the nontraditional men were likely to benefit in terms of better pay and better opportunities when compared to their female peers, but they were under-benefited compared to their male peers in traditional male occupations.

The few, or solo, men in female occupations tend to assume work roles that support their masculine identity. The male nurses, for example, specialize in work tasks in which they minimize the need for direct interaction with the patients; the men specialize in anaesthesia, emergency room, or intensive care nursing, where they work as experts on technical machinery, not as primary caregivers. Also, it is typical that the few men who work in healthcare or other caregiving occupations are encouraged by their female co-workers to participate in trade union activities. This brings the solo men informal as well as formal esteem and clout.

The empirical study of male kindergarten and primary school teachers as well as registered nurses in the Nordic countries and the United States revealed the strong female domination in the men's professional contacts. However, their informal friendship contacts were less strictly limited to female colleagues; many men mentioned both men and women as their personal friends at work. There was also a tendency for men not to mention any personal friends among their workmates. This may tell something about the men's sense of social isolation at work. It may also be the men's consciously chosen strategy: In order to maintain collegiality at work, the men restrain from too intimate and personal contacts with their women colleagues. It can also reflect the nontraditional men's tendency to distance themselves from their female colleagues.

Usually, the men found their work interesting and challenging. This generally positive attitude toward work translated into high general work satisfaction. One reason for the high work satisfaction was that the men often had a mentor who supported and encouraged them to advance on the job and get training in new professional skills. Partly because of their maleness, special position, and greater visibility, the men receive this kind of support, which, in turn, explains why the token, or solo, men in feminine occupations tend to hold more exciting and innovative work roles. Also the male networks provide sponsorship and mentoring for the newcomers. These networks are well established among the male kindergarten teachers in Finland (Lammi, 1992).

Since the men tend to specialize in work roles in which they do not always work on an equal basis with their women colleagues, it is questionable whether the presence of a few token men in female professions is likely to change the status of the female profession, erase the female label, or increase salaries. These factors are often mentioned by the women when they welcome more men into female professions. For some men, this situation is unpleasant and stressful. The men often find themselves trapped in a double-bind situation; on the one hand, their female colleagues push them into stereotyped masculine roles, and on the other hand, other men do not take them seriously if they have chosen a career in a female profession.

What is the critical number of men that makes a real difference in female occupations and workplaces, so that the men can bring new orientations and practices into the field and not exploit their special position? Especially during early school years, the man's role as a role model has been emphasized; it is said to be important for young children to be nurtured by both men and women. This has been one of the reasons why men have been welcomed as kindergarten and primary school teachers, which has further strengthened the men's role in these institutions. Consequently, there is a need to keep a few men in the field because they have a special purpose for being there. This special role may, however, have a hidden message for the children: The male gender is more valued and more "special" than the female one. Also, the solo men's special role can arouse envy and frustration among the female colleagues. With proper workplace management, these kinds of conflicts can be overcome. In this regard, the gender dimension in nursing is less sensitive.

In general, every measure should be taken to lessen the existing sharp gender segregation in the work world. However, there are no signs that, in the near future, men would be willing in greater numbers to cross the occupational gender barrier than they are today. Rather, it seems that only some individual men take this opportunity. The material and social benefits for men from crossing over are smaller than for women. In the future, women will be the ones who more actively challenge the occupational gender barriers, especially in the fields of higher formal education and specialized training.

References

Barnett, R., Bienir, L., & Baruch, G. K. (1987). *Gender and stress*. New York: Free Press.

Brown, R. G. S., & Stones, R. W. H. (1973). *The male nurse* (Occasional Papers on Social Administration, 52). London: G. Bell & Sons.

Bureau of Labor Statistics, U.S. Dept. of Labor. (1992). *Employment and earnings, 39*(1), 185-190.

Carlsson, M., & Bergknut, E. (1988). *Manliga sjuksköterskors syn på sitt yrke* [Male nurses view their work] (FoU-Rapport Nr 2/1988). Uppsala: Vårdhögskolan (in Swedish).

Epstein, C. F. (1970). *Woman's place: Options and limits in professional careers*. Berkeley: University of California Press.

Epstein, C. F. (1988). *Deceptive distinctions. Sex, gender, and the social order*. New York: Russell Sage Foundation.

Erngren, E-L., Birath, A., & Linberg, L. (1986). *Vart tar de manliga sjukskötarna vägen?* [Where do the male nurses go?]. Röda Korsets Sjuksköterskola (in Swedish).

Fottler, M. D. (1976). Attitudes of female nurses toward the male nurse: A study of occupational segregation. *Journal of Health and Social Behavior 17*, 99-111.

Freudenberger, H. J., & North, G. (1985). *Women's burnout: How to spot it, how to reverse it, and how to prevent it*. New York: Doubleday.

Gilligan, C. (1982). *In a different voice.* Cambridge, MA: Harvard University Press.

Gilligan, C., & Pollak, S. (1988). The vulnerable and invulnerable physician. In C. Gilligan, J. V. Ward, & J. M. Taylor (Eds.), *Mapping the moral domain* (pp. 245-262). Cambridge, MA: Harvard University Press.

Gutek, B. A. (1985). *Sex and the workplace: The impact of sexual behavior and harassment on women, men, and organizations.* San Francisco: Jossey-Bass.

Haavio-Mannila, E. (1989). *Miesten ja naisten työ, elämäntyyli ja hyvinvointi* [Men's and women's work, way of life, and well-being] (Research Report No. 43). Helsinki: University of Helsinki, Department of Sociology (in Finnish).

Haavio-Mannila, E. (1990). Men's work and women's work. In M. Manninen & P. Setälä (Eds.), *The lady with the bow: The story of Finnish women* (pp. 125-133). Helsinki: Otava.

Haavio-Mannila, E., & Kauppinen, K. (1992). Women and the welfare state in the Nordic countries. In H. Kahne & J. Z. Giele (Eds.), *Continuing struggle: Women's work and lives in modernizing and industrial countries.* Boulder, CO: Westview.

Haavio-Mannila, E., Kauppinen-Toropainen, K., & Kandolin, I. (1988). The effect of sex composition of the workplace on friendship, romance, and sex at work. In B. A. Gutek, A. H. Stromberg, & L. Larwood (Eds.), *Women and work* (Vol. 3, pp. 123-137). Newbury Park, CA: Sage.

Haavio-Mannila, E., Kauppinen-Toropainen, K., & Kandolin, I. (1991). Työyhteisön sukupuolijärjestelmä [Gender system of the working life]. *People and Work, 5*(3), 185-196 (in Finnish with English and Swedish summaries).

Hayes, R. (1989). Men in female-concentrated occupations. *Journal of Organizational Behavior, 10*, 201-212.

Kadushin, A. (1976). Men in a woman's profession. *Social Work, 21*, 440-447.

Kanter, R. M. (1977). *Men and women of the corporation.* New York: Basic Books.

Kauppinen, K., Haavio-Mannila, E., & Kandolin, I. (1989). Who benefits from working in non-traditional workroles: Interaction patterns and quality of work. *Acta Sociologica, 32*(4), 389-403.

Kauppinen-Toropainen, K. (1987). Ainokaiset työyhteisössä [Tokens in the work community]. *People and Work, 1,* [supp. 1] (in Finnish).

Kauppinen-Toropainen, K. (1991a, September 2-3). *Comparative study of women's work satisfaction and work commitment: Research findings from Estonia, Moscow, Michigan, and Scandinavia.* Paper prepared for the UNU/WIDER Research Conference Gender and Restructuring: Perestroika, the 1989 Revolutions, and Women. WIDER, Helsinki.

Kauppinen-Toropainen, K. (1991b). Miehet naisvaltaisissa ja naiset miesvaltaisissa ammateissa: Ainokaisaseman analyysi [Men and women working in opposite-sex occupations: "Solo" or token dynamics and job satisfaction]. *People and Work, 5*(3), 218-238 (in Finnish with English and Swedish summaries).

Kauppinen-Toropainen, K. (1991c). Työuupumus hoitotyössä miehillä ja naisilla [Burnout: Exhaustion, hardening and lack of job satisfaction among men and women doing intensive patient work]. *People and Work, 5*(3), 275-294 (in Finnish with English and Swedish summaries).

KAISA KAUPPINEN-TOROPAINEN and JOHANNA LAMMI   111

Kauppinen-Toropainen, K. (1992). *Miehet naisvaltaisten alojen työntekijöinä—ainokit, suosikit ja vuorovaikutuksen piristäjät [Men as "cheerleaders" on female-dominated jobs]*. Finland: Ministry for Social Affairs and Health, Equality Publications Series C:4, 41-46 (in Finnish).

Kauppinen-Toropainen, K., Haavio-Mannila, E., & Kandolin, I. (1984). Women at work in Finland. In M. J. Davidson & C. L. Cooper (Eds.), *Working women* (pp. 183-208). Chichester, UK: John Wiley.

Kvinnor och män i Norden [Women and men in the Nordic countries]. (1988). Facts on Equal Opportunities 1988. Nord 1988:58. Stockholm: Nordic Council of Ministers (in Swedish).

Lammi, J. (1992). *Miehet naisvaltaisissa ammateissa* [Men in female-dominated occupations]. Finland: Ministry for Social Affairs and Health, Equality Publications Series C:7 (in Finnish).

Lapidus, G. (1988). The interaction of women's work and family roles in the USSR. In B. A. Gutek, A. H. Stromberg, & L. Larwood (Eds.), *Women and work* (Vol. 3, pp. 87-121). Newbury Park, CA: Sage.

Liljeström, R. (1981). *Könsroller och sexualitet* [Gender roles and sexuality]. Stockholm: Liber (in Swedish).

Lindgren, G. (1983). *Könssegregering i arbetslivet och "kvinnlig" heterossocialitet* [Gender segregation in the worklife and "female" heterosociability]. Umeå Universitet (in Swedish).

Lipman-Blumen, J. (1976). Toward a homosocial theory of sex roles: An explanation of the sex segregation of social institutions. *Signs, 1*(3), 15-31.

Maslach, C., & Jackson, S. E. (1986). *Maslach burnout inventory manual* (2nd ed).. Palo Alto, CA: Consulting Psychologists Press.

Österberg, C., & Hedman, B. (1989). *Women and men in the Nordic countries*. Copenhagen: Nordic Council of Ministers.

Riska, E., & Wegar, K. (1989). The position of women in the medical profession in Finland—Integration or separation. In R. Silius (Ed.), *Women in male-dominated occupations*. Publications from the Women's Studies Center at the Åbo Akademi. No. 5, 14-52 (in Swedish).

Robinson, B. E. (1979). A two-year followup study of male and female caregivers. *Child Care, 8*(4), 279-294.

Rosby-Björkquist, E., & Knutsson, G. (1986). *En jämförande studie mellan manliga och kvinnliga sjuksköterskor i vårdarbetet* [A comparison between male and female nurses at work]. Örebro: Högskolan (in Swedish).

Sandnes, A-L., & Tanem, T. (1991). *". . . Frederick Nightingale, I presume?" En undersökelse blant mannlige hjelpepleier* [A study of Norwegian male auxilary nurses]. Oslo: University of Oslo, Institute of Psychology (in Norwegian).

Silius, H. (1992). *Den kringgärdade kvinnligheten* [To be a woman lawyer]. Ekenäs: Ekenäs Tryckeri Aktiebolag (in Swedish).

Sverdrup Berg, T. (1980). *Mannlige studenter og förskolelärare i studium og yrkesliv* [Male preschool teachers and students at work and at school]. Bergen: Bergen Lärerhögskole, Förskolelärareavdeling (in Norwegian).

Taeuber, C. M., & Valdisera, V. (1986). *Women in the American economy* (Current Population Reports, Series P-23, No. 146). Washington, DC: Government Printing Office.

Ve, H. (1992, June 1-2). *Gender differences in rationality, the concept of praxis knowledge and future trends.* Paper presented at International Conference on Gender, Technology and Ethics, Luleå, Sweden.

Walsh, M. R. (1977). *Doctors wanted: No women need apply.* New Haven: Yale University Press.

Wharton, A. S., & Baron, J. N. (1987). So happy together? The impact of gender segregation on men at work. *American Sociological Review, 52,* 574-587.

Williams, C. L. (1989). *Gender differences at work: Women and men in nontraditional occupations.* Berkeley: University of California Press.

Women and men in Finland. (1991). Helsinki: Central Statistical Office of Finland.

Yoder, J. D. (1985). To teach is to learn: Overcoming tokenism with mentors. *Psychology of Women Quarterly, 9,* 119-131.

7

Male Elementary Teachers

Experiences and Perspectives

JIM ALLAN

Men are currently a minority among schoolteachers in the United States. While women make up a majority—70%—of all schoolteachers nationally, gender disproportions are especially striking at the elementary level (kindergarten through sixth grade), where men currently comprise only 12% of the work force. In addition, within the K-6 grade sector, most men teach in upper elementary classrooms (grades 4-6), or work across grades in art, music, or physical education. Men teaching in the primary grades (K-3) are rare indeed, perhaps no more than one in five of the 12% total. Large elementary schools with only one male classroom teacher are not unusual. On the other hand, men continue to hold 70% of positions as elementary school principals. Data from National Education Association *Annual Estimates of School Statistics* reveal that these proportions have remained relatively stable over the past 30 years in the United States, in spite of initiatives to increase the proportions of both women administrators and men in teaching (NEA 1958/1959, 1991/1992).

In this chapter, I present a perspective on men who are elementary teachers, based on evidence from guided collaborative interviews. Between the fall of 1989 and December 1990, I conducted in-depth interviews with 15 men currently employed as elementary teachers in Iowa. Because they are few in this occupation stereotyped as "women's work," their gender as it relates to their job qualifications becomes a prominent consideration. Men who are elementary teachers are aware of others' attention to their maleness, as well as of others' conflicting expectations and stereotypes of them as men.

I explore two themes that emerged regularly in interviews. The first is the question of gender advantage for men in elementary schools. Most of those interviewed perceive encouragement from within the profession, as well as from the public, simply because they are men. But their status as tokens or minorities among the majority who are women teachers puts them in a contradictory position. On the one hand, they may form gender alliances—because they are men—with male administrators, but at the same time experience challenges of professional ineptitude—again because they are men—from women colleagues. On the other hand, they may form professional alliances with women colleagues, based on shared interests, access to power, and experiences, but are then seen by male administrators as unreliable or threatening "gender renegades."

Second, I explore some ways men negotiate these contradictions, working at constructing masculinities appropriate to the job and congruent with others' conflicting expectations. They must assert—and especially model—"being a real man" in ways that are personally sustainable, that have integrity, and that are also acceptable to those who evaluate them on this important job criterion and control their careers. At the same time, they feel pressure to conform to stereotypically feminine qualities to establish the sensitive, caring relationships necessary to effectively teach children. For these men, gender is highly problematized, and they must negotiate the meaning of masculinity every day.

Theoretical Background

The most substantial and widely publicized research on men as elementary teachers over the past 30 years derives from psychological perspectives considering, first, differing effects of male and female teachers on children's socialization, and second, the relative masculinity of men employed as elementary teachers (e.g., Sexton, 1973). Both questions proceed from unsound bases in sex role theory (Carrigan, Connell, & Lee, 1987; Pleck, 1980). Empirical research in these directions arrived at early dead ends (surveyed in Gold & Reis, 1982). Nonetheless, extensive attention to this research in professional education and popular media has legitimated persistent "folk theories" or commonsense public understandings of men in elementary teaching.

Widespread public acceptance of sex role theory, theoretical and empirical limitations notwithstanding, is reflected in commonsense "explanations" of men elementary teachers. One hypothesis may be stated thus: "A few good men in this work are 'real men' who are relatively unmotivated to teach and relatively insensitive to children—compared to women—but who are temporarily willing to 'serve time' in the classroom to qualify for competitive advantage in the more gender-appropriate work: the higher status and power positions of administration." The complementary alternative of this folk theory is: "Other males in this position may be sensitive to the needs of children and find fulfillment in 'women's work,' but are (it must follow) effeminate or unmasculine." Such folk theories of hyper- and hypomasculinity conserve the concept of exclusive sex roles by ignoring the actual lived experiences of men who do this work.

An alternative perspective on "doing" gender explores the extent to which, for individuals, it is not fixed, but relational, negotiated, and varying with time and social context (Pleck, 1980), a kind of unacknowledged "work" (West & Zimmerman, 1987). Recent studies of masculinities explore their variety and fluidity as problematic cultural constructs (Brod, 1987; Carrigan, Connell, & Lee, 1987; Kimmel, 1987). As studies of gender minorities in other occupations have suggested, what is of interest from this perspective is not degrees of deviance imputed to minorities, but the ways by which minorities redefine and maintain gender identity. Thus, Williams (1989) compared women marines and men nurses, discovering important similarities and differences between the strategies men and women adopt as minorities. In both cases, Williams discovered that gender minority workers did not conform to popular folk theory that explained their exceptionality by imputing to them characteristics of the "opposite" gender. Rather, she found internal occupational segregation, which in a variety of ways preserved or exaggerated gender identity. As a result, the creation of hyperfemininity and hypermasculinity within occupational ranks did not so much attenuate the gender stereotype of the work, as it reinforced and maintained traditional gender differences.

This current research on men working as elementary teachers is informed by the second theoretical tradition. It examines men's perceptions of others' expectations about masculinity in this profession. These perceptions, in turn, shape how men behave, justify their behaviors, and negotiate masculinity, while engaged in "women's work."

Advantages and Disadvantages
of "Being a Man"

The fact that men are especially underrepresented in the elementary sector of the teaching profession offers them both advantages and disadvantages related to their gender. In this chapter, I focus on the importance of gender in hiring decisions. Many of those I interviewed perceived that men received preferential treatment in hiring. Some remembered job interviews in which principals told them outright they were particularly interested in hiring men.

> When I went to college, I heard that superintendents wanted and needed male elementary teachers. Talking to principals, they told me they *needed* more male teachers in elementary schools. (Ross, sixth-grade science teacher)

> Going into the interview for elementary education, I was more sure of myself, from all the people telling me that you're . . . you have a good shot at getting this job because you're a man. . . . I was more confident going into elementary teaching being a male. It's just what everybody's been telling you. (Curt, fourth-grade social studies teacher)

> I had an interview just this last spring in the Chicago area where that was, I think, one of the main aspects. The woman principal told me there were no males in the school and they felt it was important to hire one. (Tom, 17-year veteran art teacher)

Three sets of reasons were offered to explain this apparent preference for men in elementary school teaching. Respondents claimed that men were preferred due to (a) their institution's commitment to affirmative action; (b) the desire of male principals for male companionship and support; and (c) the public's demand for male role models in the classroom. I will discuss each of these reasons, focusing on the contradictions they create for male elementary school teachers.

The first reason given for the preference for men was the institution's commitment to affirmative action or principles of "gender fairness." They compared their elementary school's initiative in hiring men to programs aimed at increasing women's participation in traditionally male occupations or to the hiring of racial or ethnic minorities. Some went further in suggesting that the purpose of affirmative action in hiring men was to *prove* something: to "show kids that a man can do this work." They implied that behind affirmative action was the objective of enlarging children's understandings of opportunities in the world of work, in addition to combating gender stereotypes.

As a second explanation for the apparent preference for men, some respondents suggested that elementary school principals—the majority of whom are men—seek gender alliances in otherwise all-female institutions by hiring other men as teachers. This is particularly the case when principals and male teachers share an interest in sports or a background in coaching. Men in this situation implied that a shared socialization in sports and male teamwork assures principals of male friends as well as male allies and assistants, whose loyalty, authority, assumptions, and tacit understandings they can count on. Duane, a sixth-grade math teacher and high school coach, in his 18th year of teaching, explained:

> Administrators are looking for male teachers. We had 200 applicants for three jobs in this district with only a handful of males. And those men were looked at a little bit longer in the interviewing process. My administrator told me that male teachers are easier to get along with, more receptive to administrative decisions, a little bit easier going, not liable to get as excited as easily . . . that's why he was looking. . . . Now that's not true in every case, I'm sure. . . . I think administrators feel some pressure from the public that they would like to see possibly more male influence. I think the public would like to see more men at all levels. . . . A lot of administrators are ex-coaches. They relate to men. There's a tendency to hire somebody that you can relate to. In my case, the day I interviewed, the principal was a coach at the time I was playing for a nearby college. The first half of the interview was spent discussing basketball in the sixties. You know there's kind of a bond there that develops.

Where a bond of common interest and experience existed, particularly in sports, men elementary teachers formed special relationships with male principals, often socializing together in the principal's office or the lounge as part of their daily routine. Thus, men teachers themselves perceived both affirmative action and stereotypically masculine interests male teachers shared with principals as giving some men an initial advantage in being hired.

However, this hiring preference for men was often accompanied by conflict with the female staff. Some men reported that women colleagues questioned the qualifications of men who appear to have been hired—whether through affirmative action or because of shared interests with principals—"just because they are men." The men felt challenged to prove to women the sincerity of their motivation, their aptitude for teaching, and sensitivity in human relations. Curt, the fourth-grade teacher who was also a high school coach, put it this way:

> I think sometimes female teachers will look at you, especially at first, and say, "Okay, let's see if you as a male can handle this." Especially me being a coach. And I don't know—they never said anything to me, but they kind of look at you like "are you going to be able to handle this situation?" . . . It's kind of a challenge to me. I want to show them that I can. I'm a competitive person.

Bill, a fifth-grade science teacher, one of two men working in a school with 20 women colleagues, saw a clear connection between his interest in athletics and "prejudgment" on the part of some women colleagues:

> When I started in elementary education I was the only male teacher, and my reactions were always looked at a little differently, and they were judging me, I think, a little differently because I was a man. They wanted to see how I would handle the young kids' emotions . . . or if I'd be too macho. You know, I've had contact with a number of prejudging teachers as I've entered the field as an elementary teacher. . . . People think the reason I'm doing the teaching is because I'm in athletics, and I think I've proven myself, at least in this school system, that my first priority is teaching. I *love* to teach.

Thus, the very reason for their advantage in hiring (their masculinity) raised suspicion and doubt on the part of some female teachers about the men's ability to do their job.

Some men recounted experiences that indicated to them women colleagues' opposition in principle to men teaching young children. Bill described such an encounter with a senior woman colleague at an end-of-the-school-year party:

> She finally just said, "You know, I do not believe in men in the elementary ed system. I truly just, I see no purpose for men in this part of the system." And I was offended at that point, and then she said, "But you've been able," she said, "I'm impressed. I've got to say you're an exception." Now, I was both pleased to hear that comment, complimented by it, but I was offended that she had stereotyped me, that she didn't feel men should be in that realm of teaching. She truly did not feel there was a place for men in elementary ed.

David, a fifth- and six-grade team teacher who at first had been the only male teacher in his building, recalled what he perceived as women colleagues' perplexity and suspicion:

[What do they suspect you of? What do you have to prove to them?] You're not making enough money, for one thing. Men are "supposed" to make more money. You don't know how to interact with people. You don't have people's emotional needs up front as your consideration. You don't have enough rapport with parents—this, I think is often an attitude. You really don't have the people skills to be working at the elementary level . . . you aren't smart enough. [Okay. So these are things you feel you have to prove?] Yeah. If you're a male in the first place, some women view you not exactly as a threat, but as a fish out of water. "Why are you teaching in grade school?" This has been a female domain, and it really still is. And you're suspect just because of your maleness. Well, just the way females are suspect at the university level. Their femaleness is suspect. They aren't objective enough, or they're not intelligent enough or something. . . . It's like being black in the white world. [Okay.] That sort of isolation that you are, you're not self-defined. You are defined by the environment and by the women in the environment.

Although women teachers do not control hiring, they have considerable influence on persistence. Since teaching on the elementary level requires a high degree of flexibility, collegiality, and cooperation, men who don't "prove themselves," or don't "get along," don't get rehired.

[Anything else that might make an unfortunate situation for beginning male teachers?] The ability to get along with the other teachers, the women teachers. That's a big item. You've got to be able to work together. You've got to be willing to take your place and follow suit. (Mark, third-grade teacher)

[Tell me about this man who was not rehired.] The biggest thing was not getting along with other staff members. He got off on the wrong foot with some . . . mainly women. They didn't like him; he didn't like them. . . . They let him go. (Curt, fourth-grade social studies teacher)

[How do you avoid offending them (women teachers)? How important is that for a man?] If you are going to survive in grade school! Yeah, nobody ever talks about that. I don't think, from what I've ever heard, that anyone acknowledges to undergrads in ed school that this sort of thing exists. . . . But it's absolutely essential. . . . Your edges get ground off if you're going to survive. (Steve, a fifth-grade teacher, one of two men working in a building with 26 women colleagues)

Thus two advantages men perceived in getting hired—affirmative action and interests shared with principals—were accompanied by initial disadvantages in establishing the trust and cooperation of women colleagues, which men saw as essential to success. Men are placed in a double bind: While their presumed "masculine" interests in sports and male bonding may have given them initial hiring advantages, these same characteristics can alienate men from their female colleagues.

However, not all the men interviewed experienced preference in hiring or close bonding with their male principals once on the job. Some encountered ambivalence and conflict, especially if they asserted professional autonomy or questioned school procedures. Mark, a 41-year-old teacher with 15 years of experience in elementary schools, discussed his experience with "patronizing principals":

> Generally the principals I have worked with, well, they all have been male except one. The women didn't really do this sort of behavior, but I think some men who become principals get into it because they want the authority and the power and the privilege of dominating other people. . . . It's more of a power issue. So what I've seen go on is the "rooster in the hen house" sort of thing, where you have the one special male and a collection of women. And even if the teachers are men, they are treated like women. . . . [Have you had other experiences that would add to my understanding of this?] Right. Whenever I question this principal, or I'm thinking of another male principal, at a staff meeting, there would never be agreement. Whatever I would say would be viewed as a disagreement or a threat. Whereas a woman could get away with it. With some of the principals there is never the freedom to question their judgment in public. . . . [Do you think other men also perceive this about principals as "rooster in the hen house"?] Definitely! Absolutely. I don't know how they would word it, but they would work around to it. . . .
>
> [What is the principal thinking if he finds men a threat to his authority, but he is hiring them?] Well, I think it's the same way that you hire blacks. You don't have a choice. You have to hire them because of affirmative action or it's just a politically correct thing to do. You can't avoid it. You just have to do it.
>
> [What kind of a man would your principal prefer to hire?] Someone who doesn't question his authority, even in private.

In the above example, female teachers are preferred because they are supposedly more docile and tractable than men. Male teachers can represent a threat to the authority of the male principal, especially if they ally themselves with their female colleagues. Stan, a fifth-grade teacher with 7 years of experience, after one year at a new school where he is the only male, concurred:

On all-school policy issues . . . I think my principals expected teachers to just accept the announced policy and go along, don't expect teachers as a matter of course to engage in debate. I think it's very much my business and something I should have input on. This causes more conflict for me than some women teachers because they're more apt not to speak up, even though they too may disagree. . . . My women colleagues were intimidated, I think, and I was supposed to be too. There was a lot of discontent in the staff. But I was the only one to speak out. I spoke out as a professional, but I got a lot of resistance. Now I'm more apt to keep my mouth shut and just go along. Why fight it?

Thus, being male is a potential source of simultaneous advantage and disadvantage within the gendered structure of power in elementary schools. Men elementary teachers, in forming alliances either with male principals or female colleagues, present an implicit challenge to institutionalized relationships between men and women. Men perceived themselves surrounded by conflict in structures of authority and control. Gender alliances with male administrators were offset by challenges to men's legitimacy as teachers, posed by women, who, as a majority, defined work norms and to some extent controlled men's ability to succeed and continue. On the other hand, men's discovery of and resistance to "women's work," as low-status, rationalized, and "de-skilled" labor, put them in conflict with other men who were administrators. Participants in this study revealed that *both* conflicts in the gendered structure of school authority and control were sources of frustration for them.

The third and most frequently given rationale men perceived as a hiring advantage in elementary teaching was the need for male role models for young children. Almost without exception, the men I interviewed sensed public perceptions of an important need for increased involvement of adult men in the lives of children, owing to the increasing number of single-parent families, or families in which fathers have limited interaction with their children.

I don't know what it means to be a male role model as a teacher. I say I do it, but I don't know what it means. I guess I say I do it because I have so many parents who say I do it. [Let me see if I understand. They think they need you because there isn't a father at home, and they think you're going to do something that otherwise a father would do.] Right. [But you aren't really sure you're doing it?] Right. [But they're hiring you to do it and valuing you for doing it?] Right. Yes, absolutely. (Mark, third-grade teacher)

[You sense that others, particularly parents and administrators, expect you to do something called male role modeling?] Yes. And I don't think that those parents or administrators have a clear view as to what they want. Their perceptions are, "We've had a traditional family pattern that looks like this. We don't have that any more, but we *should* still have it." . . . You see more and more studies, children born into single-parent families are much more likely to be poor. Are much more likely to have emotional problems. Much more likely to have discipline problems at school. A lot of these things. And I think this is the one thing a principal or whoever is hiring can have control over. "Well I can hire a man. I can't do much else. But perhaps hire a male and maybe that will magically help alleviate things." (Mike, a young, unmarried, "Talented and Gifted" teacher)

Thus, many men felt they were given a hiring preference because of the public's demands for more male role models, but were at a loss to identify exactly what this work consisted of.

This reason for the preferential treatment of men placed them in a very paradoxical position. For even as they were expected to be male role models, they were simultaneously stereotyped as feminine—because of the kind of work they do. A recurring theme among the men I interviewed was their awareness of public perceptions, shared in some cases by women colleagues at their level and by male colleagues at higher grade levels, that teaching children was not an occupation a competent "real man" would willingly choose. Steve, a fifth-grade teacher expressed this view:

[I want to return to your comment that elementary teachers are perceived as being feminine. You believe that there is such a public perception?] Oh, there *is*. [There's no question in your mind about that.] Oh, no. I mean it's like saying George Bush is the President. [What does that mean, being more feminine?] When men do what women usually do, people think it's a sissy activity. [How does that perception affect you?] I think you just develop a thick-skinned attitude. What makes me angry is not so much this perception, as the low status and pay associated with work women typically do.

This public perception is a deterrent to men teaching in the lower school grades.

[How would it be different for you if you were teaching in first or third grade rather than in fifth?] It would be tough for me. Maybe that's where the stereotype comes in. It would be hard for me. I guess it's not that I couldn't relate to the kids. I've taught them in summer school. I know I *can* teach them.

But I'd have a difficult time. [Why?] People look at a male first-grade teacher as being a little bit . . . *different*. You know what I mean. Family acquaintances might see this as strange. [So it would be difficult for you to work at that level?] Oh, yes. Very difficult. (Duane, veteran fifth-grade math teacher)

Females are the motherly type that can get down with little kids, but males seem like . . . some of the men don't want to admit that they can go down to that level. That's what I feel from some of the people in town. I don't know if it's ego or what. . . . Sometimes males have the feeling that they have to act like a male; it's society's expectation, and you have to be tougher and stronger—handle big kids and big discipline problems. I think some men might *want* to. I think there are male teachers who would want to. But they won't, because of the reactions they expect from other people. (Curt, fourth-grade social studies)

The men in my study used different strategies to negotiate this paradox. Some responded to the feminine stereotypes by defining their work as different from "what women do." Duane, the fifth-grade math teacher who also coached high school sports, noted that being a coach, because of the association of athletics with masculinity, helped men establish their legitimacy. But he sensed that for others, the feminine stereotype was problematic.

[Are there things that if a man is *not* a coach, but he wants to be a successful elementary teacher and get along, that he can do that give him the same kind of entry?] He had best not be the least bit feminine. I mean they expect a male teacher to be a man, whether he is a coach or not. If a man were perceived as feminine, I'm sure it would be a problem. [Why?] You need to be a male role model. Be the opposite of being feminine. Now that's pretty subjective. I guess I see it as a man who is willing to be involved in male-related activities. That is not to say that involvement in female-related activities is wrong . . . but sports, fishing, rather than cooking. I don't think it's wrong to do the cooking and things that are traditionally feminine, but yet the kids need foremost from you the male . . . the traditional male-type things need to be more preeminent.

But if a man emphasized masculinity *too* much, then he would undermine his legitimacy as a teacher. So, in addition to demonstrating stereotypical male attributes, men elementary teachers felt challenged to show sincere motivation in working with children, and sensitivity to children's limitations and needs.

[Do you detect any assumptions parents or others may have about you before they get to know you?] Well, maybe thinking a male is more of a disciplinarian. Maybe they might think that I'm meaner. Maybe they don't think I'm as sensitive. Maybe they think sometimes a man is not as sensitive as a woman . . . . Then you've got to prove to them that you're just as sensitive as the female. [Sensitive?] Yes. Like in "I care about kids' problems." (Curt)

Many men who successfully modeled what they perceived to be expected male attributes sensed fear, uncertainty, and intimidation in children, which they needed to work consciously to overcome. Yet, ways of demonstrating sensitivity that are "natural" and available to women are foreclosed for men.

At this age, kids hug more. They go up and hug their female teachers more. [Than they do the male teachers?] Yes. And I don't really mind that, because they tell us not to even show any affection, because nowadays people think a man is molesting kids if it happens. And . . . but it hurts. You see a little kid going up and hugging one of the women teachers and you're saying, "That'd be nice to get that hug," because it makes you feel better. Then they'll come up and they do surprise you and hug you and you feel better about it. (Ross, a beginning fourth-grade teacher)

It seems to me easier for a woman teacher to become involved in and comment on a child's emotional state, than it is for men. It's easier for a woman to be more supportive than it is for a male. [Are you saying that in dealing with children's emotional issues, men feel more constrained?] More constrained, *definitely*. Both can tell when a child is upset, but the male's range of appropriate responses is narrower. . . . An example is on the playground when a child is hurt. A male teacher in contact with a child . . . those gestures are always smaller. They convey just as much meaning, but they can't be on the same scale as a female's. (Mike, "Talented and Gifted" teacher)

Men felt they must overtly demonstrate care for children and sensitivity to their emotional needs. But behaviors, that are perceived as natural demonstrations of these qualities in women, are off-limits to men, who feel them as equally natural but as inviting suspicion of abuse. The vehemence with which men expressed this constraint was surprising. One participant recalled the indelible impression of his first awareness of this danger to men in elementary teaching.

I had a mentor in college, and he told me one time, I remember our conversation about my decision to change my major to elementary education. He cautioned me in a very serious manner about what devastation it could have on my career if this ever happened to me. [If what ever happened?] If there were any false charges against me in regard to sexual molestation or anything. And I had to be really careful of it, and that I needed to think of that. . . . I don't know why he told me this, but it had an incredible . . . I've never forgotten the conversation. And I have a policy. I never touch a girl unless it's on the top of the head. I never touch them. I never touch them anywhere. I never even hand them anything. . . . Boys, I don't have any rules about boys. . . . I don't have any concerns there, but the girls I do. I used to resent it, but now I just see it as a sort of fact of life—never let a girl stay after school alone. If I'm taking kids home, make sure I leave the boys off last. You know, just normal precautions. (David, fifth and sixth grade)

Several men were fearful about demonstrating caring or giving special attention to children.

[To what extent do you think men elementary teachers become aware that when they give extra attention, or whatever the child needs, that that can be misconstrued?] Oh, *definitely*. It's much easier for a woman to give a gift to a student and not have it misinterpreted. . . . I read about people losing jobs. I used to have kids sit on my lap, little kids. I don't touch anybody now, and I know this other man I work with is very much the same way. [So this has definitely constrained your practice.] Absolutely. It puts a real cramp on the teacher-student relationship. And women don't have to be afraid of that. [How do you feel about not being able to touch kids as a teacher?] I guess I haven't touched anybody for so long that I don't think about it anymore. But I had to consciously, oh, maybe 10 years ago, step back, very . . . very consciously stop doing certain things. [You never give a child a hug?] No. Especially not if I was a single man. (Terry, fourth-grade social studies teacher)

Young single men, whose time and energy are not shared with their own children, and who might therefore have more enthusiasm for as well as commitment to children at work are particularly suspect.

[How is being an elementary teacher different for a single man and a married man?] You need to be a lot more careful as a single man. All grade school men have broken the male stereotype somehow. [Married men, because they have a spouse, give more assurance? They're not going to be risky with children?] Right. Definitely. (Duane, fifth-grade math)

Parents are generally more leery of male teachers. If this was a young woman staying after school [to offer special help or extra activities], it would be no big deal at all. She would be "dedicated." "Isn't this great? She's willing to give this time, and do these things, clubs and athletics, and so forth." But this young single guy, who does a great job, he should be commended for all the time he is putting in. But it makes people a little nervous. (David, fifth- and sixth-grade team teacher)

Nearly all men interviewed perceived male role modeling as an unwritten but crucial component of their job description, a widely held expectation and criterion of success. Many men were uncertain, when asked, how to role model beyond "doing what men do." They sensed others' conflicting definitions of the male role itself: the disciplinarian surrogate father engaged only in "unfeminine" activities, or the feminine, nurturing, empathic companion of children. The men in this study were forced to steer a course between these two equally dangerous extremes, either of which could result in suspicions and ultimate dismissal. The man who is too "masculine" would be suspected of being an incompetent and insensitive teacher, while the man who is nurturing and empathic would be stereotyped as feminine and "unnatural." Thus, paradoxically, an initial hiring advantage to men carries with it certain disadvantages, insofar as it places men in an untenable situation.

Conclusion

In spite of the initial advantages offered by affirmative action, welcoming male principals, and widespread public perception of the need for more male role models in the socialization of children, men who choose elementary teaching experience stressful disadvantages, posed by conflict and contradiction focused on their maleness. In fact, each advantage is itself potentially a disadvantage or source of uneasiness.

If men are hired simply because they are men, they raise suspicions among their female colleagues about their suitability as teachers. Conversely, some men encounter hostility from male principals, who perceive male teachers as a threat to their authority. Forming alliances with either the male principal or the female teachers entails high potential costs—all because these are men working in female-identified jobs.

The hiring preference based on the need for male role models also presents a series of dilemmas for male teachers. Conforming too closely to traditional definitions of masculinity again raises doubts about men's competence as teachers, while emphasizing nurturance and sensitivity opens men to the charges of effeminacy, or even worse.

The elementary school is a thoroughly gendered institution in which being male or female is an unspoken basis of power (Apple, 1990;

Clifford, 1989). Understanding the organization of schools and the lives of those who work in them requires analysis of what Hansot and Tyack (1988) called "the absent presence" of gender: "organizational cultures in which many gender practices are implicit (often all the more powerful for being taken for granted)." Proportions of men and women in both elementary administration and teaching are particularly skewed, compared to middle schools or high schools. Men elementary school teachers often feel isolated and vulnerable, because they upset the gendered ordering of the institution. These interviews suggest that the fewness of men contributes to both their advantages and disadvantages. Future research might explore the extent to which disadvantages so outweigh advantages that men are, in effect, forestalled or forced out, thus conserving the current division of labor.

References

Apple, M. W. (1990). *Teachers and texts*. New York & London: Routledge & Kegan Paul.

Brod, H. (1987). The case for men's studies. In H. Brod (Ed.), *The making of masculinities: The new men's studies*. Boston: Allen & Unwin.

Carrigan, T., Connell, B., & Lee, J. (1987). Toward a new sociology of masculinity. In H. Brod (Ed.). *The making of masculinities: The new men's studies*. Boston: Allen & Unwin.

Clifford, G. J. (1989). Man/woman/teacher: Gender, family, and career in American educational history. In D. Warren (Ed.). *American teachers: History of a profession at work*. New York: Macmillan.

Gold, D., & Reis, M. (1982). Male teacher effects on young children: A theoretical and empirical consideration. *Sex Roles, 18*(5), 493-513.

Hansot, E., & Tyack, D. (1988). Gender in American public schools: Thinking institutionally. *Signs, 13*(4), 741-760.

Kimmel, M. S. (1987). Rethinking "masculinity": New directions in research. In M. S. Kimmel (Ed.), *Changing men: New directions in research on men and masculinity*. Newbury Park, CA: Sage.

National Education Association. (1958/1959-1991/1992). *Annual Estimates of School Statistics*. Washington, DC: Author.

Pleck, J. H. (1980). *The myth of masculinity*. Cambridge: MIT Press.

Richardson, J., & Hatcher, B. W. (1983). Feminization of public school teaching: 1870-1920. *Work and Occupations, 10*(1) 81-98.

Sexton, P. (1973). *The feminized male: Classrooms, white collars and the decline of manliness*. New York: Random House.

Strober, M., & Tyack, D. (1980, Spring). Why do women teach and men manage? *Signs, 5*, 494-503.

West, C., & Zimmerman, D. H. (1987). Doing gender. *Gender & Society, 1*(2), 125-51.

Williams, C. L. (1989). *Gender differences at work: Women and men in nontraditional occupations*. Berkeley: University of California Press.

8

Male Secretaries

ROSEMARY PRINGLE

Two years ago I was appointed to a promotions committee at a provincial university. Complicated travel arrangements had to be made each time for the 12 or so out-of-town members, and there were difficulties finding dates that were mutually compatible. Extensive documentation had to be collected and circulated, interviews arranged, referees contacted. At each meeting Pat, the secretary, not only took minutes but frequently left the room to make telephone calls and send faxes. Pat's role was clearly to do the bidding of the chair. Pat did all this cheerfully and was warmly thanked by members of the committee at the end for taking care of them. The work was secretarial in the broadest sense, including organizing lunches and daily travel arrangements, and helping to clear the cups away after morning tea. But Pat was a man. And nobody thought it at all odd that he should be doing this work. It was, after all, a high-level, confidential committee chaired by the Vice-Chancellor. Pat was a besuited, slightly swarthy man in his late forties, not in any way effeminate. He was doing work that was clearly defined as appropriate to a man, and he was formally classified, not as a secretary but as an administrative officer.

Pat is not unique. Every large organization has dozens of men like him, performing a similar range of tasks to those done by female secretaries, often under the direction of a "boss" and often, as in Pat's case, including a range of semipersonal services. Rather than being called secretaries, they are generally classified as clerical, administrative, or even managerial workers. At the same time, male secretaries are thought to be few and far between. The media have found novelty value in such role reversals, and have posed the question of whether, in response to feminist demands for equality in the workplace, men will return to secretarial work, perhaps serving women bosses. It is important, therefore, to consider the relationship between the minority who are labeled "male secretaries" and the much larger group who are doing broadly secretarial work.

This chapter derives from a larger study, *Secretaries Talk* (Pringle, 1988), based on historical and statistical data, census returns, representations of secretaries in the media and in student text books, and interviews with both secretarial and nonsecretarial workers in a range of workplaces, large and small, government and nongovernment. While the material on which I draw is mostly Australian, similar processes have taken place throughout the Western industrialized world (Benet, 1972; Crompton & Jones, 1984; Davies, 1982; Kanter, 1977). Some variation can be expected at the level of the region, the firm, and the individual. It will be argued that while there are key discourses that structure secretaries' working lives, these discourses are not imposed in a deterministic way. Rather, they exist as frameworks of meaning within which individuals negotiate their relationships: There is room for different outcomes and for shifts in emphasis. Though male secretaries were sought, there are only 7 in the sample of 149 secretaries interviewed for *Secretaries Talk,* and most of these were found only after I eventually stopped asking for "male secretaries" and substituted job profiles (Pringle, 1988, p. 271). Once I began to realize how the categorization was limiting the data, it became relatively easy to locate men doing broadly similar work. Had I started doing this earlier, I might well have included a higher proportion of men. This is indicative of the extent to which occupational groupings, which at first seem self-evident, are shaped by the categories that are used to organize them. The emphasis on gender polarity can mask a great deal of common ground between men's and women's work. It was thus not only the changing labor process of secretarial work that needed to be studied but also shifts in its definition and meaning.

Feminist Approaches

Feminist scholars have provided a clear outline of the processes whereby secretarial work, which until the third quarter of the nineteenth century was done almost entirely by men, came in the twentieth century to be perceived as quintessentially women's work. Once an apprentice-ship for management, or a way of learning the business before taking it over, secretarial work changed dramatically as the result of both new office technology and the growth of a more complex corporate econ-omy. Middle management expanded, opening up new opportunities to men who might once have been clerks and simultaneously creating new low-status keyboard and stenographic positions that were filled by women. Secretarial work became mechanized and deskilled, and no longer served as a gateway to power. The sexual division of labor was redefined to include a sharp differentiation between secretarial jobs on the one hand and administrative and managerial jobs on the other. Work has continued to be organized around gender polarities, with clear-cut distinctions between men's and women's work. As argued in *Gender at Work*, gender is not only about difference but also about power: the domination of men and the subordination of women. This power rela-tion is maintained by the creation of distinctions between male and female spheres (Game & Pringle, 1983, p. 16). Not only are jobs defined according to a clear gender dichotomy, but the gendering of jobs has been important to the construction of gender identity. Gender is not constructed in the family and then taken out to work but is continually reconstituted in a number of arenas, including work. Men need to experience their work as empowering. Performing secretarial work, as it conveyed ancillary service functions carried out by women, was increasingly seen as a threat to masculine power and identity.

One of the limitations of such an analysis is that it assumes that both occupational and gender categories are empirically given. It will be argued here that neither occupational titles nor gender labels merely describe a pregiven reality, but exist in discourses that actively consti-tute that reality. Discourse is precisely this—the ways of understanding, interpreting, and responding to a "reality," which it is impossible to know in any other way. This is not to imply that reality does not exist—in this case, substantial differences in the tasks performed by men and women. But occupations do not emerge straightforwardly from an observation of the labor process. These occupational divisions could equally well have been described in a number of other ways and need not have assumed a gender polarity. In any case, secretaries are not sitting at their desks waiting to be counted. Their numbers vary enor-mously, depending on which meaning is being produced: In Australia it could range between 25,000 and a half million, depending on whether one wanted to differentiate between executive assistants and routine filing clerks. It is notable, too, that secretarial work is still routinely described in terms of individual boss/secretary relationships, even though such relationships are now largely restricted to senior management (Pringle, 1988, pp. 174-194).

If we cannot take occupations as given in reality, neither can we take gender as given. Kessler and McKenna (1978, pp. 102-103) point out that by assuming in advance the centrality of gender categories, we inevitably reproduce such categories. The possibility of describing social relations in any other way is then systematically excluded, and gender is presented as fixed and given. Most questions posed about gender assume a sharp dichotomy, that is, that everyone fits one and only one category, and that one's gender is invariant. On the contrary, they suggest, it is "our seeing two genders" that leads to the "discovery" of biological, psychological, and social differences. They argue for a more open approach, suggesting that if gender is a social construction, it might be treated as more fluid. Judith Butler has made the case against essentialism even more strongly, arguing that gender coherence is a regulatory fiction (1990, pp. 329-339). She rejects the assumption that individuals have a deep psychic investment in gender identity, socially constructed or otherwise, and insists that this is imposed purely through discourse.

While Butler's anti-essentialist position is extreme, it does open up new ways of thinking about gender and occupations. It calls into question the deep connections between gender and occupational identities and suggests that it may be possible to resituate the issues. The subject of male secretaries is a particularly promising area to investigate this approach, for it poses the contradiction between men's horror of being labeled "male secretaries," while they are willing to do the same or very similar work as long as they are not so labeled. Why does a simple change of label make it acceptable? On the one hand gender seems so rigid that secretarial work presents a threat to a man's core gender identity. On the other, it may be relatively straightforward to resituate the subject in a different occupational discourse, recasting the "reality" in a different frame. The question that needs to be raised is not, why there are so few male secretaries; but rather, why the title "secretary" is reserved almost exclusively for women, and how it affects the negotiation of workplace identities and power relations.

What Is a Secretary?

It is impossible to answer the question "what is a secretary?" by describing what a secretary *does*. If it were so, the many thousands of Pats in existence would surely be included. There are actually a range of discourses, statistical and cultural, in which meanings are produced about what a secretary *is* (Pringle, 1988). We come to know secretaries and to identify them as a group through the ways in which they are represented. This is true of all groups, but in most cases the emphasis is on the actual work and the social relations surrounding it. A plumber, or for that matter a stenographer or typist, does not have a particularly strong cultural presence. By contrast, the secretary is constructed in popular culture in a way that plays down the importance of what she does, in favor of discussion of what she is. Secretary is one of the few employment categories for which there has never been a clear job description. Secretaries do a wide variety of things, and there is not even one task, such as typing, that we can confidently say they all perform. This ambiguity about what constitutes a secretary's work makes it easily available for cultural redefinition. Secretaries are part of folklore and popular culture and are represented in stereotypical ways in advertising and the media, even in pornography.

In the twentieth century secretaries have come to be defined first as exclusively women, and second in familial and sexual terms. If, as the psychoanalysts suggest, woman is perceived as lacking what it takes to be a man, so secretaries were assumed to lack the qualities that make a successful boss. The equating of secretary with woman or wife, and boss with man, has been important in establishing the normative versions of what a secretary is. So powerful are these norms that female bosses and male secretaries are perceived as out of step, and the relationship may be difficult to read in traditional boss/secretary terms—it may simply be perceived as two people working together (Pringle, 1988, pp. 82-83).

The question "what is a secretary" may be answered with reference to three discourses, which have coexisted at times peacefully and at others in open competition with one another. The first of these, the "office wife," emerged early this century and had its origins in the debate about whether (middle-class) women should work outside the home. It may be found in serious journals, teaching manuals, and the practices of a good many secretarial studies teachers, as well as the more traditional bosses and secretaries. It signified that women's primary place was in the home, that her other tasks would be redefined in relation to this and restricted to support roles. The two main requirements of the office wife were that she be deferential and that she be ladylike. The office wife is portrayed as the extension of her boss: loyal, trustworthy, and devoted. Though the discourse has been modernized, debate about changes in secretarial work is frequently cast in terms of how far office marriages are changing. Are they being transformed into more companionate and egalitarian relations, where the wife might have other interests or refuse to do certain aspects of the housework?

By the 1950s the prim, spinsterish figure with the bun had been challenged by alternative images, appearing regularly in tabloid cartoons, of the blonde "dolly bird" figure, with large breasts, long legs, and short skirts. Where the office wife had been a workhorse, putting order into the office, the dolly was presented as a source of chaos and diversion. The office wife is subservient, passive, and reserved; but the dolly is cheeky and loud and is represented as having an active sexuality and a degree of sexual power over the boss. What the two had in common was their definition in gendered and familial terms. Secretaries could be wives, mothers, mistresses, dragons, or spinster aunts.

A third set of meanings has struggled to emerge, which resists the familial and sexual definitions, treats secretaries as having serious careers, emphasizes skill and experience, and plays down the special relationship between boss and secretary in favor of viewing both as part of a management team. Although this "equal opportunity" discourse gathered strength by the 1970s, and proclaimed that gender should not be important in the construction of occupational categories, the earlier meanings live on and need to be addressed seriously in the discussion of work.

The inclusion of a sexual dynamic in the boss/secretary relationship has largely excluded men from being defined as secretaries. It would be tantamount to declaring both boss and secretary to be gay. Male secretaries are often assumed to be gay. This is both a conventional way of interpreting a male sexuality that is perceived as lacking power and a statement about the place of sexuality in people's perceptions of the boss/secretary relation. Alternately, male secretaries may be incorporated in familial terms as sons and brothers. (Sons who are currently performing filial duties but will, in the course of time, move on to establish their autonomous place in the world.) In the fantasies of women managers, male secretaries may at times appear as toy boys and playthings—but significantly *never* in the powerful subject positions of husbands or fathers. I shall return to these questions, drawing on interview data, in the final section.

Shifting Definitions of Secretaries

The history of men and women in secretarial work must take account of not only technological and organizational change, but also shifting frameworks of meaning. Far from being a fixed, identifiable group, secretaries are a fluid and shifting category; and sociologists, economists, journalists, managers, clerks, keyboard operators, personal assistants, and so on, may have quite different notions of who should be included. The changing definitions of secretaries are amplified by the decisions of the statisticians as to how to count and classify them. Official statistics are no more neutral a discourse than any other; they too produce specific meanings for *secretary*. This section looks at the ongoing presence of men in secretarial work since the late nineteenth century, and the ways in which that presence has been discursively disguised, particularly by statisticians who have interpreted the occupational structure in ways that emphasized sexual polarities.

Even though in the nineteenth century secretaries were men, it is now assumed that secretaries have been women since time immemorial. Secretarial work is now seen as so traditionally women's work that it is hard to remember how recently this work has become feminized. Although in the United States women began to move into secretarial work during the Civil War period, it was not until about 1930 that a clear majority of secretaries were women, and not until the 1950s that male secretaries began to seem strange or unusual (Benet, 1972; Davies, 1982). In the space of a very few decades, the secretarial workforce underwent a sex change. This feminization occurred in conjunction with a major shift in the meaning and status of *secretary*.

The shift is signified by the three definitions offered by the *Oxford English Dictionary* (1979), which will be discussed in turn. The first of these definitions invokes the older meaning, which lives on in titles like Secretary of State or Press Secretary.

> One who is entrusted with private or secret matters; one whose office is to write for another, especially one who is employed to conduct correspondence, to keep records and (usually) to transact other business for another person or for a society, corporation or public body.

It usually appears in capitals and still signifies largely male preserves. While the British Foreign Secretary and the American Defense Secretary are there to serve a monarch and a president, respectively, they exercise enormous power. Men who are Secretaries in this earlier sense are often impatient or uncomfortable about comparing themselves with "small s" secretaries. Had anyone used the word *secretary* to refer to Pat, they would have implicitly added, "in the old sense," more akin to a company or union secretary than to somebody who served a boss.

The second Oxford definition indicates a transition of meaning:

> Private secretary—a secretary employed by a minister of state or other high official for the personal correspondence connected with his official positions. Also applied to a secretary in the employ of a particular person (as distinguished from the secretary to a society, etc).

As assistants to senior managers, private secretaries still act as officers of the company or organization, but their continuity with secretaries in the earlier sense goes largely unacknowledged and they are, for counting purposes, usually included with typists and stenographers.

The third definition more accurately conveys what most contemporary secretaries do and is indicative of the shift to "women's work":

> A person employed to help deal with correspondence, typing, filing and similar routine work.

Historical Transitions

The changes signified by the dictionary definitions did not take place overnight but happened gradually over half a century. They are linked to major changes in the occupational structure and the development of new tiers of clerical work, made possible by new technologies. This section attempts a broad periodization from the 1890s, when the first two definitions still held sway, to the developments since World War II, when the third definition became the most widely used one.

1890–1920

Of all the components of what is now called secretarial work, telephony was the first to be designated as feminine (Kingston, 1975, p. 93). Typing was initially considered to require not only manual dexterity but also some practical knowledge of the material being processed (Fitzsimmons, 1980, p. 24). It was therefore perceived as appropriate work for men. As typewriters came into general use, in the first decade of the twentieth century, and the demand for operators increased, typing became accepted as a women's subject. Shorthand retained a masculine image, but had, before World War I, become paired with typing by employers to create the feminine job classification of "shorthand-typiste." The first two national censuses in Australia replaced "secretary" with "officer in a public company," a small group which remained predominantly male. Typists and stenographers were included in the general categories of "office caretaker, keeper, attendant" and "clerk, cashier, accountant undefined." The proportion of women in the latter category rose to 35% by 1921 and, when this is checked against the job advertisements for the period, it is reasonable to assume that many of them were typists, stenographers, and private secretaries.

1920–1945

Though men continued to engage in secretarial work in the inter-war period, their proportion steadily declined. The feminine "typiste" came to be used in the job advertisements of the 1920s to distinguish "women's work." The statisticians caught up with this terminology and, in the 1933 census created the gendered category "typiste, office machinist," from which men were absent by definition. Until World War II advertisements for typists (without the "e") still routinely appeared in the classifieds, which indicates that a number of men were employed as typist/clerks. The majority of secretaries, as distinct from stenographers, were also still men. But for the male secretaries, unlike most of the women, stenographic work was the start rather than the end of a career. The key way that young men without a tertiary education could get promotion in the public service, for example, was by going to night school and studying either shorthand or accountancy. Shorthand was taken as a kind of alternative evidence of intellectual ability. Even in the 1980s there were senior male public servants and company managers who had started their careers as stenographic and secretarial workers (Byrne, 1982, p. 10).

Late 1940s–Present

In the late 1940s the term *secretary* began to be used more loosely in the classifieds to describe what had previously been understood in more precise terms as stenographers and typists. The statisticians were obviously concerned that company secretaries might get confused with humbler typing varieties. "Secretary" disappeared entirely as a census category. Rather than making any effort to distinguish private secretaries as a professional group, they collapsed them into the category of "typists and shorthand writers." From a masculinist viewpoint it was convenient to do this because they then did not have to identify or acknowledge levels of skill. "Women's work" could be seen as an undifferentiated category of unskilled labor.

In the 1947 census men were again counted among typists and stenographers, but their numbers were small: 245 out of 71,000. Although officially gender-neutral, the "typist, stenographer" category was treated, by the statisticians, as a feminine one. The coders were actually allowed to take gender into account in deciding how to categorize people. Men who did shorthand or typing (and there were still a large number of them in the public service) were thus recoded as clerks. If "shorthand typist" was a category reserved for women, so too was "receptionist." So that there could be no mistake about this, the 1976 and 1981 censuses actually labeled the group "receptionist, female." A man, by definition, could not be a receptionist and would have to be placed in some other category.

As a result of these processes, men in secretarial work became literally invisible as "secretaries" and were treated as part of a clerical and administrative work force with a separate career path. Male secretaries gained novelty value. Newspapers have loved to "discover" the occasional "brave" man who is attending secretarial college. In Australia, they have been discovering him every few months since at least 1968! (*Sun-Herald,* November 10, 1968). In 1973, when employers faced the prospect of equal pay, we were told that Caulfield Institute had just enrolled their first male in a secretarial postgraduate course (*Australian,* March 4, 1973); that Stella Cornelius (furrier and arbiter of women's fashion) had a male personal assistant (*Sydney Morning Herald,* March 14, 1973); and that such men were earning nearly twice as much as the women and saw their jobs as stepping-stones to more important careers (*Sydney Morning Herald,* February 7, 1973). After equal pay for work of equal value became official policy in 1975, the popular press threatened that "the first male secretaries are sharpening their pencils to lead the men's lib march down the corridors of power" and that they were "edging out boardroom blondes." One of their number allegedly commented: "Female secretaries are two a penny. Men beat them for efficiency and stability. . . . We don't fall pregnant and don't come and go" (*Sun-Herald,* January 9, 1977). A year later it was "Take a letter MR Jones" (*Sun-Herald,* March 5, 1977). In 1982 a policeman was chosen as Queensland's Secretary of the Year: As the *Herald* put it, "Sergeant Greg takes on the girls and cops it sweet." He had started 20 years earlier as a foot patrolman and gone on to become assistant to the police commissioner. With admirable secretarial tact, he commented: "The police in Queensland have received a lot of unwarranted criticism lately and I hope my award can do a little bit to help our cause" (*Sydney Morning Herald,* April 22, 1982).

The strong associations of "secretary" with femininity and sexuality have a number of implications for men doing broadly secretarial work. Currently, men are rarely called secretaries. They are generally described as assistants of some kind, or as computer operators, clerks, or trainees. As late as 1970 a textbook for secretarial students noted that:

> In industries where secretaries are required to represent their employers, in factories or on construction sites, and in strictly masculine provinces, male secretaries are in great demand . . . they are frequently employed in the legal field, in purchasing, mining, the oil and rubber industries, public utilities and in the newspaper field. (Solly et al., 1970, pp. 6-7)

Men continued to use stenographic skills in the armed forces, the police, and journalism. The State Rail Authority insisted that its junior recruits learn to type, and in the 1960s still required shorthand as a qualification for its clerks. Court reporting also remained a male preserve, although women had taken over the typing side. In what seems a strange division of labor, the reporters took down the proceedings in shorthand and dictated them directly to typists. Men only dropped out in the 1980s, when the work apparently became less attractive to them after equal pay was implemented (Pringle, 1988, p. 170). While the number of men doing secretarial work has undoubtedly dropped, a number remain who are simply not perceived as secretaries because of their gender. As a result, the extent to which secretarial work has been feminized has been overemphasised.

"Male Secretaries"

While the majority of men in secretarial work are not called secretaries, a few are quite self-consciously given that label, and it is necessary to ask why they have been singled out in this way, rather than incorporated into an "assistant" category. According to my research, men labeled as secretaries are often thought, by those with whom they work, to have some "problem" with their masculinity. Said one manager:

> I had a male secretary once. He was a clerk who came from the Air Force and I discovered one day, quite by accident, that he wrote shorthand and he typed. . . . I didn't have a secretary at the time and he was one of those guys who was quite happy to fill a secretarial role. . . . He was an effeminate sort of person and he appeared to enjoy the subservient role. He was one of those people who always wanted to help you.

The boss's assumption appeared to be: What "real" man would want to be subservient, let alone helpful! Male secretaries may also be sensitive to assumptions made about their sexuality, as another interviewee insists:

> An old retired bloke comes in regularly to relive the old days. . . . The other morning he came in. He stopped and he looked at me and I was typing. And I was aware that he was looking at me . . . and he said, what's your name, Miss? And I looked at him and said, it's Jacqueline, actually! He didn't get it. He just sort of grunted and walked off.
>
> I don't object to having overtones of femininity. I mean, everyone's got their yin and their yang. But the implication in a male-dominated society, and particularly in the last bastion of male domination . . . is that femininity is associated with homosexuality, which is taboo . . . which conjures up all sorts of nasty images. So that's what I cope with every day.

Any "feminized" occupation is presumed to draw homosexual men: Fashion, hairdressing, entertainment, and more recently nursing are cases in point. A firm connection is made between gender and sexual preference, and the stronger the sex-typing of the job, the stronger the resulting stereotype. The popular press reinforces such connections, for example, by seeking out gay secretaries. The Sydney *Sun-Herald,* for example, in an article titled "Sex Changes in the Typing Pool" (July 1982), described the unhappy experience of Ashley, before he joined the safety of the public service: " 'It was disastrous', he said. 'The boss tried to chase me around the desk. I left after only three-and-a-half weeks.' " The passage probably says more about the fear expressed by the interviewer, of what happens to men in an occupation that is not only subordinate and feminized, but perceived in such strongly sexual terms. The sexuality of the boss is not problematical here—he is represented as sexually dominant and willing to take sexual liberties with the secretary, regardless of either gender or sexual preference.

Ashley *was* actually gay (I interviewed him 4 years later) but he is in the minority. In my research it was easier to find gay nurses than gay secretaries; and even in nursing, gays are a minority. Gay secretaries were largely a newspaper fiction of the 1970s and 1980s. There is no reason to believe that gay men are congregated in secretarial work. A gay lawyer, with a high proportion of gay clients, told me he had advertised widely for a male secretary and had not been able to find anyone suitably qualified. He thought the legal profession was probably too staid for such people. A spokesman for the Gay Business Association in Sydney suggested that gay men may perceive secretaries as "dowdy," and the work as involving long hours of drudgery. He suggested that they were more likely to be working as receptionists or switchboard operators than as secretaries. Secretarial work does not necessarily represent femininity for gay men. In some cases it may represent the opposite. The only other gay secretary I interviewed grew up in a country town and wanted to be a court or Hansard reporter, he explained, to reconcile his sexuality with "something masculine." When he did not get the necessary speeds, he joined the State Rail Authority, which had also retained a masculine image, and it was only when he became dissatisfied with the promotional prospects there that he became willing to consider more stereotypically secretarial positions in the private sector.

The media discourse about gay male secretaries now seems a little dated, particularly since the emergence of "gay machismo." Since the mid-1980s more women have moved into senior executive positions (particularly in the public service) and often find themselves dealing with male subordinates. These women often joked to me about the "male secretary" as a subject of titillation, a possible object of desire or a status symbol (a toy boy or a handbag). Given the notorious difficulties that women bosses often report with female secretaries (Pringle, 1988, pp. 57-83), a male personal assistant has both practical and erotic appeal. To reverse the master/slave relationship is to represent the woman as both powerful and stylish. It is to imply that she is cared for by a man, who both finds her sexually attractive and admires and respects her, offering the same kind of loyalty that men have in the past extracted from their female secretaries. It is also to exploit the traditionally higher status of the manservant or butler over the female domestic (the status of male secretaries might be lower than that of men in many other occupations, but they are likely to earn more than their female counterparts). The numbers of female boss/male secretary pairs are not vast, but their appearance in the discourse of women managers is indicative of a shift in the way male secretaries are being regarded. It is notable that they continue to be sexually defined, though in new ways. Perhaps because of this sexualization, most men doing secretarial work still express discomfort at the prospect of being labeled "male secretaries."

Male Bosses

Some male managers said they "could not imagine" having a man as a secretary, and it is quite possible that male applicants face discrimination. One of my subjects recalled that when he was living in London two other men he knew were "temping" for solicitors and found it very difficult to get work "until they had tried them once. And it took 3 or 4 months for these guys to get established. It is a very staid industry." To many male bosses the relationship with a "secretary" is of an intimate nature and is more appropriately with a woman. Yet managers are constantly in the position of supervising those below them in the chain of command. Why should it be so different in principle when the person concerned is a "secretary"? As soon as the person concerned is renamed an "assistant" of some kind, the problem appears to go away. A professor spoke warmly of his "technical officer," who, "to my delight writes letters almost in the words I would have used." He relies on him for "higher level secretarial tasks" and sees a future for a lot more men in these positions.

Bosses may deal with the sexualization issue by denying that their male secretaries are secretaries or by treating them differently. One senior manager commented:

> A male secretary . . . would not be called my secretary but my assistant. . . . I think I would get a male secretary to do additional work because he was male. . . . Simply because other males here that are helping me, the marketing manager, the accountant, the product manager . . . are doing work of a particular level. . . . I would imagine this guy taking on more and more responsibility and then one day I would say, "Why don't we get a typist?"

Once appointed, male secretaries appear to receive very favorable treatment and the "discrimination" works to their advantage. In a rather similar way male doctors, embarrassed by the sexual connotations of the doctor/nurse relationship, often treat male nurses as junior doctors, explain more processes to them, and facilitate their speedier progress through the system (Game & Pringle, 1983, pp. 110-111). Since it is "unimaginable" that men might be secretaries, they tend to be paid more and to move quickly up the career ladder.

Male secretaries earn about 20% more than their female counterparts, a figure that directly parallels the differential for full-time workers overall (Pringle, 1988, p. 171). The self-confidence and assertiveness of the two male secretaries discussed below thus has a solid financial basis. The higher rate cannot be explained in terms of the different occupation distributions of men and women, and can only signify that the men are receiving more favorable treatment and moving into personal assistant positions.

Family Games

Where male secretaries are not defined sexually, they may be integrated, in family terms, as brothers or sons. Tim, for example, works in the family law firm. He tells close friends that he is a secretary but otherwise describes himself as a legal clerk. He picked up typing while working in a bank and works from Dictaphone. He does not take shorthand. His brother and sister, both solicitors, say he is the best secretary they have had because he wants to know exactly what each piece of work is about. He behaves as though he were one of the legal staff and, like many other male secretaries, is treating it as a stepping-stone. He is currently taking an accountancy course.

Phillip Warton works for a family-based pharmaceutical company, where he is treated by both husband and wife as the son. While this has its frustrations, particularly with the wife, it also gives him a stronger power base than that usually available to sisters or daughters. Phillip agreed to talk to me after a woman friend of his saw my advertisement for "male secretaries" and volunteered him. He had not identified himself as a secretary until that time because his description says he is a "marketing assistant." Now in his early 20s he had started work in a bank and had taken it upon himself to learn to type when he found he kept making mistakes on bank cheques and international drafts.

> I went to tech for 6 months and learned to type. . . . There was two other guys there but it was very sexist actually in that the woman who was teaching me to type came to me and said that I didn't have to bother too much about spacing

and those aspects of typing because I wouldn't be using that in my role. And I said, but if I was going to be a secretary I would. She said, "But you're not—what are you doing it for?" She automatically presumed I was not going to be a secretary. . . . I didn't have to do typing tests on spacing and setting out letters and what have you. I just went strictly on speed typing.

He earns 30% to 40% more than he was getting in the bank. Despite his lack of a science or pharmacy degree, he is being groomed for a long-term position in the company. But he does not see a future in it, and it is unlikely that he will stay. Phillip has taken the job to get marketing experience and plans to do a marketing diploma. How does he describe his current job?

Basically it is to look after the managing director. I run after him, and organize him, keep his desk tidy, make sure he goes to appointments. . . . Get things done that he should do and doesn't get time for.

But he is always introduced as "my assistant," my offsider, Phillip who runs around after me . . . never as secretary. Phillip claims a degree of power in relation to his boss:

I think he feels, not threatened by me, but I feel I have the ability to tell him what to do. I tell him what to do and he does it. I'll go in there and I'll say, "Your desk is utterly disgusting. How can you find anything?" And I'll come back into his office and there will be piles on the floor for me to take away to file. His wife thinks it's wonderful that he's got me to run around after him. . . . But in regard to a power play he's still M.D., and he knows he still is . . . and knows that it's just a game. . . . Sometimes I feel like that and other times I feel he's a bit wimpy, because someone who's only been in the company for 3 months has the ability to say something to him.

It was unusual to hear female secretaries talk like this in an interview situation, regardless of what they might have felt privately.

Though he replaced a woman who did a lot of typing, Phillip rarely uses his typing skills at work. He says:

. . . The only time I'll type is if I need it and there's no one to do it. I've heard it said that the girl that is doing the typing now has had to do more because I'm there. . . . Mind you, typing was a stipulation of the job . . . but he [the boss] didn't even ask me if I could type . . . he just assumed I didn't.

And I said to him, "You didn't ask me about typing." He said, "Do you type?" I said, "Of course I do, I did a tech course." "Oh, really? That's an added advantage, isn't it?" I thought, oh, well, he must have taken me on on the basis of my other attributes.

This "girl" appears a few minutes later as the boss's wife and a director of the company. Her relationship with Phillip is complex. He asserts his ascendancy over her, too, as the typist who lacks many of his skills, but at the same time he regards her as the power behind the throne.

So you give typing to her?
    Yes but it doesn't work that way because she . . . is not the typist. She is a director and she will take time out.

As the interview continues, her authority increases rapidly. She controls the office, keeps everything under surveillance, and basically manages things. If there is conflict between her and her husband, she gets her way. She intervenes on every level. She insists on a high standard of dress and routinely comments on Phillip's ties, clothes, hairstyle, and so on. At first this is presented in terms of mother-son intimacy. The two of them talk about PLU—people like us. You are either PLU or you are not. But before long, he switches again and says that if he were going to resign, it would be because of her. He finds it "frustrating" that she constantly goes behind his back to the boss:

If I do something that she disagrees with . . . she won't tell me, she'll go to Douglas. And then he will ask me, "Why did you do that?" . . . Everything that goes on, she is always overseeing. If I resign from the job, it will be basically because of her. I find her a very frustrating woman to deal with. Because I cannot find my footing with her. She is not direct. She is behind my back.

Perhaps it is not accidental that Phillip's own mother had been a secretary and in all likelihood intervened in similar ways in his relationship with his father.
    Phillip's role is considerably more high profile than that of the "girl" he replaced. He does no routine typing, and as a result the boss's wife, herself a director and actively engaged in managing the company, takes on additional typing work. A conflict ensues in which she is constantly putting him in his place, showing that ultimately it is she rather than he who will have her way with Douglas, the patriarch. He can be the favored son only by conforming to her whims, and he has made the judgment that his future will be better served by moving on.

Gender and Power

Clearly, gender does alter the boss-secretary relationship. Raoul, unlike Phillip, is actually defined as a secretary and is thus placed at a cultural disadvantage, subject to ridicule. Yet he is able to develop strategies of asserting masculine power. His boss, Geraldine Milner, is a senior manager with a large merchant bank, for which she has worked for the past 15 years. Her main responsibilities are with advisory services and public relations. She is 41 and single. Beyond that she revealed virtually nothing about her private life.

Though very aware of the problems of being a woman in a male-dominated industry, she does not attach any significance to having a male secretary. I asked her what she thought about the common view that it would be hard for men to be in those sorts of support positions:

> Rubbish! What a load! Have they ever tried it? I mean, this is it! It's crazy! I've always had men working for me and I haven't noticed any difference. . . . I've never really expected my secretaries to get my cups of coffee or cups of tea or anything like that . . . if that's what they term support. . . . I suppose some men expect their secretaries to go out and buy their wives' birthday presents and all that sort of nonsense. . . . I would never consider asking them to do anything other than what was required in a professional capacity.

Her secretary, Raoul Wicks, is 26 and single. He was dressed in a crumpled suit, which barely fulfilled the formal dress requirements, and he appeared to thumb his nose at the style associated with merchant banks. Having dropped out of a Bachelor of Business degree halfway through, he has had a rather checkered career as an actor and odd-jobs person. He is in this position rather accidentally, having originally contacted the bank about another clerical job.

Geraldine stressed there was no difference between what Raoul did and what previous female secretaries had done:

> I want someone who can do the basic school lectures for us. Someone who can handle the phones and preferably who knows the industry, at least enough to answer a lot of the basic queries. I don't really have sufficient typing and normal things like that to warrant a full-time secretary.
>
> Raoul's here because he studied and wants to work in the industry, so it's a very good training position for someone in the long term. Another former secretary has now gone into a broker's office and is doing extremely well.

Raoul, on the other hand, is not happy about being called a secretary, and goes out of his way to explain why the term is inappropriate. He says that when the job was first discussed, the term *secretary* was never mentioned. They just said:

> I would need to do a little bit of typing. . . . It looked like an attractive job. There's a certain amount of prestige in working for this organization. . . . At that point in time I couldn't type but I rapidly learned. . . . I went and did one of those bloody student receptionist center courses . . .

He stressed the ways in which his job is different from that of a secretary—and went on to give what is a very typical job description:

> My job involves doing all the administration in the department. . . . I answer all the mail . . . and discern where it should go and who should answer it. If I can answer it, I answer it. I handle all the bookings for schools for our educational talks . . . for community organizations . . . and for companies. . . . I also take lectures for school and community groups. I handle all the merchandising for the department. I sell all the sweatshirts. I am in charge of the accounts. . . . I do the banking. . . . I also take phone inquiries.

"Lecturing" to school and community groups is beyond the duties of most secretaries, but it is the only task that stands out. There had been some concern to find him an alternative title, befitting his status as a male, but Geraldine would have none of this. Where his strategy of power was to emphasize his difference from secretaries, hers was to assert his similarity with his female predecessors. The connections between discourse and power are very obvious here, in the two quite different interpretations of "secretary" that are put forward as the terms of the relationship are negotiated.

On this occasion Geraldine won. As Raoul describes it:

> The personnel officer rang me. . . . She was updating the telephone directory . . . and she said to me, "Oh, Raoul, what are we going to call you? You're not really a "secretary," are you. . . you do more than that . . . how about we call you "Information Officer"? I said that's fine, that sounds good. And she said, "I'll talk to Geraldine and get back to you.". . .No more was said . . . and when the telephone list came out, there I was, a secretary and that was that. . . . I didn't say anything to Geraldine about it. I didn't feel I could.

He goes to some lengths to enlist sympathy for his "predicament":

If one wants to belong to a club, particularly a men's club, there are certain
do's and don'ts. There are certain mores, and it therefore doesn't augur well
to be a secretary. Maybe 30 years ago . . . if you had been a private secretary . . . that may have been different. . . . Now if you're doing a woman's
job, the implication is that you are somehow feminine. And femininity has
no place in a men's club.

He claims to get teased by young girls in the office who imply he is not
a proper man. And yet what comes across is the power that this man is
able to exercise. Typically, when I interviewed both members of a
boss/secretary pair, the male boss was loquacious and open, while the
female secretary was more guarded. On this occasion, the female boss
restricts her range of comments, while the male secretary talks freely,
explicitly, and quite personally about her. I did not meet a single female
secretary who talked in quite this way about a boss, male or female. On
this occasion gender clearly overrides formal position in determining
what can be said. Thus he comments:

I think she's perceived as a hard arse. But I think she's had to be a hard arse
to get where she's got to. I also think she's perceived as pretty neurotic and I
do know that she has a nickname around here.
    She gets bad-mouthed a lot behind her back. I have to be careful, as there
may be times when I agree with what people are saying. I have found myself
slip on a couple of occasions and say, yes, you're right . . . or enforce their
prejudices rather than just taking a neutral stance.
    Yes, she's perceived as being hard and tough, particularly with women.
She's tougher on women than she is on men. . . . So I think . . . you know,
jobs for the boys doesn't necessarily operate with jobs for the girls.

He talks at length about the way in which Geraldine exercises power
over him. As he talks it becomes clear that the flow of power between
them fluctuates very much more than is the case with female secretaries and either male or female bosses. He thinks she has "very
definite limits and very definite boundaries that cannot be over-
stepped," but seems to delight in playing games with them. On one
occasion Geraldine asserts her authority because Raoul has forgotten
to leave her a message. His comeback is, first, that only a woman
would be concerned with such "trivia," dismissing the possibility
that it may have been important to make every effort to return the
call. Second, he implies it is because he is a man that she has to
bother asserting herself in this way at all:

> I think she expects that she doesn't have to exert any authority with women. I mean, someone who has authority doesn't feel the need to display it. . . . With women I don't think she feels the need to display it. But with men she does have a need to display it.

Raoul continues in this vein, ostensibly describing her power and his subordination, but actually imposing his own power in the situation and reducing hers through stereotyping her—first as a dragon and then as a typical neurotic woman.

> The male bosses I have had are more even. They're less prone to ups and downs. With my boss at the moment . . . I leave her alone for at least a good hour. I've learned that now. Leave her alone till half past 10 and probably it'll be okay. But as soon as she walks in the door, the first thing I have to do is sum her up . . . and see what kind of mood she's in.

It is hardly unusual for secretaries to discern their bosses' moods, and adjust their behavior accordingly. But he turns this into a kind of reverse power base. He concedes that men's moods fluctuate, too:

> . . . but I don't think it's as visible. . . . That's kind of more dangerous because they're actually prone to exploding on you without any warning, whereas with Geraldine, I've got a pretty fair idea in advance.

He claims the power to read her accurately, literally placing her via a detailed description of her clothes. None of the women interviewed said anything like this of her boss:

> I can tell a lot from the way she's dressed. . . . There was one dress that has a very high collar . . . it's quite rigid . . . and it's pleated all the way down. . . . I know that she's in a very no-nonsense mood when I see that dress. . . . Like today we've got work to do. . . . She has a little crimson suit and that's another no-nonsense outfit. But it says . . . I'm more available today. I'm more open. I will probably be meeting executives or important VIPs. . . . There is another dress that has a split up the center, and that has its own connotations. And that's usually when she's far more relaxed. The perfume she wears tells me how she feels that day, too. So I try to sum those things up.

While Geraldine denies that the gender of her secretary makes any difference, Raoul thinks she is very aware of his maleness. Unlike female secretaries, he is quite happy to talk about sexual fantasies and interactions, assuming that he has control.

I can imagine having an affair with Geraldine. But I can't imagine having an affair with Geraldine and working here, because I just think it would just alter the relationship entirely, and it would become untenable for her and for me.

He thinks in the first few weeks in the job there was a kind of sexual attraction going on. Whether the attraction was mutual or his fantasy we do not know, but he curtailed it. As if to have the last word he says:

I've never told her when I'm pissed off, never. I think that would be to take advantage of the relationship between the sexes, so I don't. Because I couldn't do it with a man. I couldn't go to a man and say, "Look, what you have just done really annoys me," or "The way you've spoken to me really annoys me."

In other words, he believes he could take advantage of male power but claims he does not. The implication is that she depends on his gallantry and cooperation. Remembering his unease at being called a secretary, he has had to turn the situation around in fantasy, and to some extent in practice, to make it acceptable to his masculine ego. Geraldine's counter-strategy is to deny that his masculinity has any relevance to the situation and to try to ensure that it brings him no extra privileges. It is clear that, on this occasion at least, gender does matter.

Summary

The normative boss/secretary relationship involves a male boss and a female secretary. When the gender of either is changed, the relationship is quite considerably transformed. Despite stereotyping of male secretaries as "inadequate" men, they are often able to draw on images of masculine power and competence to negotiate significant power in relation to managers. While one must be cautious about generalizing on the basis of a small number of interviews, the discursive strategies that are available to men in secretarial work are fairly clear.

Men have always maintained a presence, albeit a minority one, in secretarial work; the reason this cannot be seen is because of the sexual and gendered nature of the cultural construction of "secretary." Men can and do type, though they often decline to do so at work, for fear of losing their status or their masculinity. Increasingly, managers have computer terminals on their desks, and the old distinction between clerical and secretarial work is breaking down.

The question is not how to get more men into secretarial work but the terms on which they come in. As with other areas of "traditional" women's work, the danger for women is that men will take over the best-paid, most prestigious jobs; that the division between gendered categories of work will be replaced by a horizontal division in which women are restricted to the bottom rungs. This has already happened to some extent in nursing, where men become charge nurses more quickly and move up the administrative hierarchy. But in nursing the movement of some men into positions of power has been counter-balanced by powerful unions, by strong moves toward professionalization and the upgrading of nursing qualifications. It can be argued that the presence of men has assisted in the upgrading of status and working conditions for everyone. In secretarial work the position is quite different. Outside the public sector, the unions are weak and the movement of men into the area does not signify that secretarial work is being acknowledged as professional or managerial in any genuine sense. The fact that "male secretaries" as well as female ones are so often perceived in sexual terms probably does currently limit their capacity to challenge women for many of the most prestigious jobs. While in the short term it may be to the benefit of the women that the sexual definitions are extended in this way, in the long term it will be necessary to challenge the sexualized meanings of "secretary" to ensure that it does not continue to be used to limit the areas available to women. This involves not only a change of label but also struggles around the discursive frameworks within which meanings are constituted.

References

Australian. (1973, March 3).

Benet, M. K. (1972). *Secretary: An inquiry into the female ghetto*. London: Sidgwick & Jackson.

Butler, J. (1990). Gender trouble, feminist theory and psychoanalytic discourse. In L. J. Nicholson (Ed.), *Feminism/postmodernism* (pp. 324-340). New York: Routledge.

Byrne, R. (1982). Occupation—secretary: An historical perspective. A paper presented at the seminar, Secretarial Education: A New Direction. Melbourne: Chisholm Institute of Technology.

Crompton, R., & Jones, G. (1984). *White collar proletariat: Deskilling and gender in clerical work*. London: Macmillan.

Davies, M. (1982). *Woman's place is at the typewriter*. Philadelphia: Temple University Press.

Fitzsimmons, K. (1980). The involvement of women in the commercial sector 1850-1891. *Second women and labor conference papers.* Melbourne: Melbourne University.

Game, A., & Pringle, R. (1983). *Gender at work.* Sydney: Allen & Unwin.

Kanter, R. M. (1977). *Men and women of the corporation.* New York: Basic Books.

Kessler, S., & McKenna, W. (1978). *Gender: An ethnomethodological approach.* London: Verso.

Kingston, B. (1975). *My wife, my daughter and poor Mary Ann.* Melbourne: Nelson.

Oxford English dictionary. (1979). Oxford: Oxford University Press.

Pringle, R. (1988). *Secretaries talk.* London: Verso.

Solly, E., et al. (1970). *The secretary at work* (3rd ed.) Melbourne: McGraw-Hill.

Sun-Herald. (1968, November 10).

Sun-Herald. (1977, January 9).

Sun-Herald. (1977, March 5).

Sydney Morning Herald. (1973, February 7).

Sydney Morning Herald. (1973, March 14).

Sydney Morning Herald. (1982, April 22).

Sydney Sun-Herald. (1982, July).

9

Male Elder Caregivers

JEFFREY S. APPLEGATE
LENARD W. KAYE

Perhaps nowhere in late twentieth-century society is the gendered division of domestic labor more obdurately institutionalized than in the provision of care by families to their frail elderly relatives. When an aging family member needs assistance, a female relative usually steps into the primary helping role (Abel, 1990; Finley, 1989; Sommers, 1985). Despite a dramatic increase in women's participation in the full-time labor force, and some beginning shifts in traditional gender patterns in child care, "women and men continue to accept the proposition that it is women's role to provide the day-to-day care of the old" (Brody, 1986, p. 198). Because the persistence of this arrangement has been reflected in research, what we know about family elder caregiving applies primarily to female elder caregiving. Yet at least one quarter of family elder caregivers—up to one third in some clinical settings—are husbands, sons, sons-in-law, brothers, and other men (Zarit, Todd, & Zarit, 1986).

Following a review of current trends in family elder care and of psychological, social, and structural factors that reinforce the feminization of caregiving, this chapter reports selected findings from a study of men providing primary care to an older relative. By examining the experiences of men whose lives cohere around activities that they have been socialized to view as women's work, we hope to contribute to the discourse on gender in contemporary family life.

Elder Care: The Challenge
to Changing Families

A striking convergence of demographic, political, and ideological trends presents America's more than 7 million family elder caregivers with unprecedented challenges and dilemmas. Healthcare advances and associated declining mortality rates foster the vertical expansion of more and more families into three, four, and five generations. The fastest growing cohort of older citizens is comprised of those 85 and older, the "oldest old," for whom some form of chronic illness, disability, and lingering dependency on others for their care is a virtual certainty (Bould, Sanborn, & Reif, 1989; Ory, 1985).

As the proportion of frail older people increases, however, the ranks of their potential family caregivers dwindle. A steadily declining birthrate in recent decades leaves fewer siblings to care for their oldest kin, and few adult children to care for parents (Sherman, Ward, & LaGory, 1988). Even when there are several potential caregivers in multigenerational families, one close relative is usually assigned the primary caregiving role and receives little or no assistance from others in the family system (Baum & Page, 1991). The resulting disparity between growing elder need and shrinking family resources casts a troubling shadow into the twenty-first century—especially since sharp cutbacks in formal services to the elderly reinforce the traditional societal injunction that families should "take care of their own" (Sussman, 1985).

The Feminization of Family Elder Care

Embedded in this injunction to self-sufficiency is a powerful reinforcement of women's predominance in elder care. A burgeoning literature documents that, translated into the language of day-to-day domestic life, the term *family elder caregiver* becomes a euphemism for *unpaid female relative* (Wood, 1987). Because on average women live longer than men, wives are more likely than husbands to assume spousal caregiving duties. This mortality difference also means that, in the absence of older husbands to care for their wives, the care of elderly women is more likely to fall to adult children, especially daughters (Siegel & Taeuber,

1986). Today, the average woman can plan to spend 17 years of her life taking care of children and 18 years assisting aged relatives ("Mothers Bearing," 1989). Research suggests that women give more of the personally demanding hands-on elder care than do men, whose primary functions typically include less intimate—and less stressful—tasks, such as home maintenance, transportation, and financial management (Horowitz, 1985). In general, women provide these high levels of care with little outside assistance. Among elder caregivers, wives and daughters appear to receive the fewest community services (Stoller, 1990). Enright (1991) concludes that male caregivers benefit from "the traditional gender role expectations that perceive caregiving, like child rearing, as a role in which men require more assistance than women" (p. 380).

Horowitz (1985) suggests that, in the past, women's primary roles as homemakers have appeared to afford them the flexible "free" time that elder caregiving requires. The basis for this rationalization crumbles, however, as more and more women enter the full-time labor force. Among women 45 to 54 years old—the group of midlife women most likely to be ensnared by competing demands from a husband, growing children, and an elderly relative—64% are working full-time outside the home (Schick, 1986). And these women are not cutting back on caregiving to accommodate their jobs. In one sample, while being employed reduced the amount of caregiving assistance provided by sons an average of 20 hours a month, working did not reduce daughters' assistance significantly (Stoller, 1983).

Such efforts to combine the demands of elder care with full-time employment place women at especially high risk for anxiety, depression, fatigue, reduced well-being, health problems, and other symptoms of role overload. George (1984), for example, found that female caregivers in her study took more psychotropic drugs, reported more stress symptoms, and derived less pleasure from their sparse leisure time than did their male counterparts. Apparently more taxing than the demanding hands-on work of caregiving is the interpersonal and intrapsychic toll it exacts. Feelings of anger, guilt, and remorse may intrude on previously gratifying relationships in uncharacteristic and uncomfortable ways (George & Gwyther, 1986; Zarit, 1982).

Men as Elder Caregivers

Research in the past 10 years suggests that as women reach their absorptive capacity to provide primary elder care in families, many men are becoming caregivers for aging parents (Horowitz, 1985; Stoller, 1983) and, more frequently, for spouses (Davies, Priddy, & Tinklenberg, 1986; Gregory, Peters, & Cameron, 1990; Zarit, Todd, & Zarit, 1986). Because more women than men develop Alzheimer's disease, the caregiving burdens of this latter group are especially likely to be assumed by husbands (Fitting, Rabins, Lucas, & Eastham, 1986).

As primary elder caregivers, these men navigate a course that society has left relatively uncharted. Deeply engaged in nurturant tasks and activities, they confront challenges to fundamental self-conceptions that have been shaped and reinforced by a variety of psychological, social, and structural influences. Developmental theory suggests that, from earliest years, processes related to the consolidation of core gender identity lead girls toward intimacy and connectedness with others, while fostering autonomy in boys (Chodorow, 1978). Western sex-role socialization, both at home and at school, reinforces this psychological bifurcation (Block, 1984). From her research on children's moral development, Gilligan (1982) concludes that girls' grounding in an "ethic of caring" enables them to perform caregiving tasks more comfortably and naturally than boys, whose "ethic of justice" emphasizes the objective, less contextual dimensions of relationships. Gutmann (1987) suggests that the societal imperative for young adults to reproduce further rigidifies this sex-role stereotype, engaging women in careers of caregiving at the domestic center of the family while encouraging men to "provide and protect" from a distant position at its perimeter.

Recently, scholars of the politics of family life have subjected the institutionalization of this arrangement to structural analysis. Abel and Nelson (1990), for example, assert that elder caregiving, like child care and housework, is a form of reproductive labor that serves and perpetuates the patriarchy by keeping women at a disadvantage in the labor market. As they see it, a view of elder caregiving that emphasizes the emotional rewards of caregiving has the insidious effect of "enshrining activities that are entwined with women's subordinate status" (Abel & Nelson, 1990, p. 7). Such sentimentalization conceals the grinding quotidian reality of elder care, which, like housework, is often monotonous, repetitive, and temporally unbounded, offering little sense of completion (Stoller, 1990). The work is relatively invisible, keeping caregivers hidden in a private sphere of domestic isolation that fosters exclusivity and privatism rather than collective responsibility for elder dependents.

Predictably, findings from quantitative studies that compare male to female elder caregivers appear to confirm stereotypic conceptions of gender role allocation. For example, Rathbone-McCuan and Coward

(1985) found that daughters were eight times more likely than sons to be involved in household chores and were three times more likely than sons to provide baths, toileting, and other personal care. In contrast, sons were nine times more likely to help with home repair and maintenance than were daughters.

Studies of spouse caregivers, while revealing a less distinct task polarization, suggest that men approach their responsibilities in a more instrumental, objective, and rigidly scheduled manner than do women, who have difficulty distancing themselves emotionally from their duties. Miller (1990) found, for example, that while women experience conflict in assuming authority and tend to adopt flexible, less controlled routines that leave them vulnerable to overwork, men's caregiving "may take on such workplace attributes as scheduling and hierarchy" (p. 98). Such an approach appears to insulate men from some of the guilt, depression, and other emotional stresses and burdens reported by women (Zarit, 1982). Or, as Davies, Priddy, and Tinklenberg (1986) suggest, men may learn to more successfully conceal upsetting feelings from themselves and from others.

Some small-scale qualitative studies designed to probe the subjective complexity of male caregivers' experiences reveal a less stereotypic picture than do the quantitative findings from larger comparative studies. In an ethnography of six older men caring for their severely impaired wives, for example, Motenko (1988) found that her subjects were motivated primarily by a wish to sustain the spousal relationship. They reported finding pride, self-esteem, and security in caregiving and appeared to be thoroughly identified with the primary caregiving role. Although open in their acknowledgement of stress and burden, they did not want someone else to take over. Their stress appeared to be related more to loss of the relationship with their wives than to the tedium of caregiving tasks. Although their wishes to pay back their wives for the care bestowed on them earlier reflected an ethic of justice, their approach to caregiving also expressed an ethic of caring and connectedness (Gilligan, 1982).

Such findings echo formulations by life span development theorists, who suggest that as men reach middle age, the period when they are most likely to take on elder care responsibilities, they move naturally toward a more androgynous self-definition and welcome opportunities for intimate involvement in family life (Gutmann, 1987). As a more equitable gender distribution of elder caregiving tasks becomes increasingly imperative, it is important to continue to examine male caregivers' motivations and experiences so that policies, programs, and services can respond to their unique needs.

The Study

Findings reported here emerge from a national and local study of male elder caregivers that was supported by the Andrus Foundation of the American Association of Retired Persons. Subjects were recruited from national directories of caregiver support groups.

Details of methods and findings from the national part of the study, a large-scale mailed survey of caregiver support group leaders and male participants in their groups, can be found in Kaye and Applegate (1990a). Although some summary findings from the national sample appear in this chapter, we draw primarily from findings from the local portion of the study. These findings were gathered during intensive semistructured interviews with a small convenience sample of male caregivers and the elderly recipients of their care living in the Philadelphia metropolitan area. The original plan was to interview 30 caregiver/recipient pairs. But it soon became apparent that most of the local men were caring for recipients too demented and/or otherwise impaired to be interviewed. Consequently, although all 30 male caregivers were interviewed, only 9 of the 32 recipients (two men were each taking care of two relatives) could respond coherently to questions. One of the central findings from the local study, therefore, is that most of the men were caring for profoundly impaired relatives. In one poignant example, a caregiver assured one of the authors that, although his mother might seem "a little confused at times," she would be a responsive and informative interviewee. Within 5 minutes, her responses unraveled into a rambling, tangential monologue punctuated by inappropriate laughter and other behavior suggestive of hallucinations. She was disoriented, believing that her parents, long deceased, were providing her care. Apparently her son could sustain his role as her caregiver only by marshalling considerable denial of the extent of her Alzheimer's-related dementia.

The local sample of male caregivers, demographically a mirror image of the larger national sample (see Kaye & Applegate, 1990a), ranged in age from 27 to 86 years. Half were older than 65 and another third were between 50 and 65 years old, with a mean age of 61. All but one of the caregivers were Caucasian. Half were Protestant; just more than one quarter were Catholic, 10% were Jewish, and 13% listed their affiliation as "other." The majority had finished high school, 40% had attended college, and nearly one quarter had done graduate work. Although most caregivers (63%) were retired, one quarter were working full-time. They were managing well financially, with more than 60% reporting incomes in excess of $30,000. In general, they reported "good" to "excellent" physical and mental health. Twenty-five of the 30 considered themselves to carry primary responsibility for the recipients of their care, and one third reported devoting more than 60 hours a week to their caregiving duties.

These men were caring for old, frail relatives, all but four of whom were women. Two thirds were older than 75, and another quarter were between 65 and 75 years old, with a mean age of 79. Eleven recipients were caregivers' mothers, and nine were wives. Remaining recipients included parents-in-law (five), grandparents (two), sisters (three), a father, and a great-aunt. Sixty percent of recipients had Alzheimer's disease, other forms of dementia, or organic brain syndrome. As noted, varying degrees of dementia in several additional recipients interfered with interviewing them. Consistent with this level of disability, 60% of the caregivers believed recipients' physical health to be only "fair" or "poor," and 85% thought their care recipients suffered from significant cognitive, mental, and emotional disturbance.

The Path to Male Elder Caregiving

Many of the men interviewed for the study appeared to arrive at elder care either when others were unavailable or because they wanted to avoid the upheaval and expense of nursing home placement. The following statements were typical: "Our kids don't have time, so I'm elected." "The children are all married and taking care of their own children. I took early retirement when my wife couldn't be left alone." "I wanted to save money and didn't want to pay for a nursing home and part with my life savings." The contractual strength of marriage vows was apparent; several husbands said, simply, "I'm her husband," implying that they were the only appropriate caregiver candidates. One husband elaborated: "My wife and I have been married 47 years. We've had a good life. It's the best I can do. If reversed, she'd do it for me." For others, filial duty was paramount: "Because I'm their son, that's all I can say. I fell into it by blood."

Several men expressed surprise that they ended up in the caregiving role. Asked if he anticipated taking care of his sister, one man exclaimed, "No—she was an ox! I never thought she'd get sick. I was preoccupied, in a world of my own." Another said that his wife "was the mainstay of the family; a giver, not a taker. A great person. She took care of everything." One man, banking on the predictive accuracy of mortality statistics, believed that he would die before his wife and so did not think about becoming her caregiver. Another assumed his daughter would step in to help if his wife became disabled. The striking absence of planning for the caregiver role reveals the pervasive societal assumption that men are unlikely to fill it. One of the female care recipients summed up this view concisely: "[People] look at caregiving as not being a man's job. But it's good to have them if there's no one else around."

Challenging the prevailing view that men eschew elder care responsibilities, however, a majority of our sample reported that they wanted to assume them. As one man caring for his wife explained, "I'm glad that I'm able to. I feel it shows I care about her." Some seemed to express in caregiving an ethic of rights, duty, and obligation seen as typical of men, for example: "It's the absolute right thing to do—the only thing." "It doesn't bother me. You get married; you make the vow for sickness and health." "It's my duty—a repayment for what [my wife] put up with for 50 years."

Many, however, seemed to be operating on the basis of an ethic of caring and responsibility believed to be more typical of women (Gilligan, 1982): "She's my mother and I love her. 'Honor thy father and thy mother.' " "She [mother] loves the feeling of being in her home—I want to keep her happy." "She's my wife. I feel that I owe it to her to do all I can to make her life bearable."

Although in the minority, a few men were openly resentful of becoming primary elder caregivers, characterizing the job as "a drag" or "a pain in the neck": "I'm resentful that the burden is placed on me, and I'd never do it again." "Sometimes I feel like a prisoner in my own home." But most, while ambivalent, had reached a level of acceptance and tried to find meaning in their responsibilities. One man caring for a mother with Alzheimer's disease said, "It has become my life-style. I left my job to do it because I couldn't do both. I took up a 'new ministry.' " Another caring for disabled parents declared, "I feel good about it. It's hard as hell, but I'll never have any regrets."

The Tasks of Elder Caregiving

As noted, research comparing male to female caregivers suggests that men engage primarily in emotionally distant, instrumental tasks, while women tend to offer more intimate, expressive social and emotional support. The male caregivers in the national sample did not conform to this picture. Asked to rate the frequency, competence, and satisfaction with which they performed a variety of social support, instrumental, personal care, and case management tasks, the majority of these caregivers put social support in first place. Many men in the local sample echoed this pattern. Several mentioned the salience of their role as companions, or "just being there." One man reported, "I provide her [wife] with a sense of well-being and some life enjoyment." Another saw providing "a loving relationship" as his primary activity. One man caring for his 88-year-old mother with dementia cast his caregiving role in expressive terms: "Being her son; giving her a feeling of being loved; getting her things she wants." Many seemed to find considerable satisfaction in acting as emotionally supportive companions. Reflecting on satisfying aspects of caregiving, one gentleman's response was typical: "Just being together. She [84-year-old mother] used to like to be with me, and now she has me for hours." Another, caring for his 74-year-old sister, was most satisfied "when I make her laugh, hug her, and get her dancing." Several recipients spoke of the importance of their caregivers' emotional support. As an 85-year-old woman receiving care from her son put it, "He does everything for me, but the best is that he loves me."

Indeed, many of these caregivers appeared to be doing "everything." Not confined to rating discrete tasks as were men in the national sample, local respondents offered narrative accounts that capture more fully the layered complexity of their caregiving roles. As noted in the following responses to a question about what the men did for their care recipients, tasks ranged across the spectrum of caregiving activities: "Emotional support, changing her wet bed at night, help with dressing." "Changing her colostomy bag; feeding her and giving her drinks; calming her down, holding her hand, talking to her." Some descriptions of functional tasks reflect parallels to child care. For example, one man caring for his 75-year-old wife with Alzheimer's disease said: "I change her, feed her, and put her to bed." Another husband of an Alzheimer's sufferer elaborated: "I feed her and take care of her feeding tube three times a day. I turn her [in bed] four or five times a day. I empty her catheter."

Several of the respondents derived a sense of accomplishment and pride from performing these tasks. One man declared, "I take pride in giving her [mother] medications, cooking a balanced meal, and making sure she's dressed properly." Another, caring for a mother with Alzheimer's, felt he could do "whatever has to be done. I've been shown how to do everything and I can do it all." Many talked about becoming good cooks, skillful shoppers, and capable household managers. Care recipients generally affirmed this view. One articulate woman with a degenerative disease painted a generally positive picture of her husband's caregiving competence:

> He is good at physically righting me and getting me around. He is good at dressing me. He has become a very good cook. He is a good housekeeper when he wants to be—when people are coming to visit; day-to-day housekeeping is not so good. He's particularly good at respecting my intelligence and treating me like an adult. He treats me like an equal partner on important issues that concern us both.

But for many men, a sense of competence waned when they were called into the intimate arena of personal care. This was true for both the national and local samples. With only one exception, a man caring for his wife, men in the local group felt least skillful at bathing and toileting recipients of their care. Here the gender difference became a formidable barrier.

One man believed he could do everything well, "up to incontinence." Speaking about his mother, another said, "I can't help her in the shower. She wouldn't like me to see her if she got into trouble showering." A 66-year-old single man caring for his 94-year-old mother felt impeded because he was "taking care of a woman. Not having been married, I don't do well with things like getting her dressed." Remarks by some care recipients suggested that the intimacy of marriage did make personal care less uncomfortable for husbands. While acknowledging that "at bathroom needs, women are better," one recipient qualified her opinion: "My husband is an exception; he is at ease with these things and so am I." Most recipients, however, were aware of their caregivers' discomfort: "He's a man and my son. He feels uncomfortable doing hygiene things for me." Not surprisingly, most female recipients preferred a woman for functional care. One mused, "Men are preferable for some tasks requiring strength . . . except for bathroom needs—there I'd prefer a woman." Another recipient echoed this feeling: "At bathroom needs, women are better. These needs are too personal—I am more comfortable with women."

Several comments by both caregivers and recipients suggest that, while men's sense of competence in functional caregiving may have been compromised by sex-role socialization that affords them little training and experience, they can learn if given the opportunity. One man commented, "I've gotten used to it. I feel like a male nurse. I never would have thought I could do it." Another declared, "It's not a gender difference. Women have had more experience [caregiving], but men can be as good caretakers as women." A female recipient elaborated this idea:

> My husband was a good child care person, and I guess I have become a large child. Lifting me has been easier for men. Smaller chores, women do—but women are disposed to be helpful to women. Men are less helpful with hands-on help the first time, but they get better.

Relationship Issues

As the local interviews moved from the objectivity of tasks to the more subjective world of caregiving attitudes and relationships, responses appeared to reflect prevailing views of gender differences. Asked to consider whether gender made a difference in caregiving, one man mused, "Yes, I'm probably not as good as a woman—not that intuitive, not socialized that way. Sometimes it's a bone of contention. I can appear insensitive." Another responded, "Yes, in some ways she [mother] might relate more to a woman. There are ways a woman relates to another woman that I can't do." With the exception of one man who cited "our sexist society" as the primary reason for this difference, most respondents explained it by referring to personality and socialization factors: "Women are more sensitive, men more brutal. Men try to put things out of their minds." "Women are made to have children; they learn, and it is part of their nature, to be caring."

Clearly, some local respondents appear to have internalized very traditional views of differences between men and women, including aspects of the popular rhetoric that caregiving is "natural" for women. The remarks of a female recipient, contrasting her caregiving encounters with men and women, reveal some of the nuances of gender differences:

> At first men perceive me as disabled and then change—more so than women. Women approach me more quickly and ask what they can do. They will sustain eye contact and will not be put off by how I appear. Women are more condescending, however. They will "baby down" to me in conversation.

For some men relational aspects of caring for demented recipients tried their patience and challenged their efforts to control their angry feelings. As one man caring for his wife with Alzheimer's put it, "When she gets her back up, I'm lost. You can't belt her; you just walk around and sweat. . . ." Similar expressions of pent-up anger were sometimes associated with a feeling of being trapped. One respondent caring for his 91-year-old mother declared, "It's a hassle and a nuisance. I can't get away to travel or go away for even one day." Others complained of being "tied down," of finding "no escape," of having to forfeit dreams of postretirement freedom. More than the guilt, depression, and remorse frequently associated in the literature with women's experience of the emotional stress of elder caregiving (George, 1984), feelings of frustration, irritation, and disillusionment appeared to characterize these respondents' reactions to stress.

It was neither the tedium of tasks nor the relational strains of caregiving, however, that most frequently burdened the men in this study. The majority, like the subjects in Motenko's (1988) ethnography, were most deeply distressed by feelings of loss. As one respondent caring for a wife with Alzheimer's disease confided, "You have no one to share things with any more. We used to go to restaurants together, do chores, and so forth. Now I'm by myself."

Despite these feelings of personal loss, most men attempted to make meaning of their situation through viewing it as instructive and positively challenging. Indeed, for many caregiving appeared to become a new job or retirement project, an approach that seemed to ameliorate feelings of burden. Two respondents' views were typical: "It has made me more sensitive about senior people. I'm a better person, and I apply my self-knowledge to other situations." "It's made me as complete a person as I can be. It gives you all kinds of challenges and experiences." These comments appear to support Liptzin's (1984) conclusion that "masculinity does not exclude caring that may be growth enhancing and involves as much 'taking' or benefit to the 'care-giver' as to the 'care-recipient' " (p. 76).

Discussion and Conclusion

First, it is important to emphasize that because they were recruited from caregiver support groups, the men in both the national and local samples of this study constitute an unusual group. Perhaps living out an injunction to "bear up" and keep their troubles to themselves, male elder caregivers tend not to use such services as much as their female counterparts

(Gregory et al., 1990). Generalization of findings presented here, therefore, must be limited. Nevertheless, these findings do offer some gender perspectives on men who find themselves in a nontraditional domestic role.

Despite having internalized traditional views of gender differences, these men were deeply engaged in the full range of caregiving tasks and in the relational matrix of their work. They saw their most salient and satisfying activities as the provision of social support, especially companionship and emotional sustenance. While not masking feelings of frustration and stress, most reported considerable gratification from caregiving. Given that most of the men were caring for recipients ravaged by the emotional, mental, and behavioral sequelae of Alzheimer's disease, this overall positive view suggests either extraordinary patience and acceptance or sturdy defenses—or, more likely, some combination of both. Also, several of the men appeared to find gratification in mastering challenges to their personal competence. Confronted with feelings of ineptitude in providing personal care, for example, a number of respondents became determined to learn, putting their own stamp on this activity. This proactive coping style appeared to reduce feelings of inadequacy and to preserve self-esteem.

The capacity to remain engaged in and to derive satisfaction from relational aspects of caregiving may be associated in part with a comfort with androgyny believed to become more apparent in midlife men. Asked to rate themselves on a variety of instrumental and affective personality traits, the men in the national sample chose descriptors reflecting an integration of traits; in fact, they tended to describe themselves more in affective than in instrumental terms (Kaye & Applegate, 1990b). Comments by local respondents frequently echoed this tendency. A complex combination of an ethic of caring and an ethic of justice appeared to motivate them. These findings, while more impressionistic than conclusive, suggest that although retaining traditional dualistic attitudes about gender roles, the caregivers' behavior and feelings were not rigidly sextyped. Whether these were men who had naturally become more feminized with middle age; ended up as caregivers because of a predisposition toward affiliative, expressive personality attributes; or became more affective through caregiving experiences is impossible to determine.

Our impressions of the study findings lead us to favor the latter hypothesis. For many of the men in this sample, providing primary elder care appeared to foster a sense of deep relational engagement. It seems possible that the caregiving experience may potentiate in men the expression of nurturant capacities that they have been socialized to repress, but which can be revived in various contexts. Such an idea finds support in a growing body of evidence emerging from studies of the "new nurturing father" (Applegate, 1987; Cath, Gurwitt, & Ross, 1982; Pruett, 1987). Findings from these studies suggest that men engaged in primary infant care often achieve an expanded affective repertoire and experience shifts toward a more androgynous self-conception. Primary elder care may have a similar effect.

In order to counter the pervasive androcentric bias in traditional theories of human development and personality, scholarship on gender in the past two decades has focused on highlighting difference and explicating women's unique experiences. As noted, from this work emerges a conception of women as grounded in connectedness while men are seen as valuing autonomy and separateness. Newer formulations offer a more complex, integrative picture. Bergman (1991), for example, explores the dynamics of "men-in-relation," suggesting that "Men as well as women are motivated by a primary desire for connection" (p. 1). This suggestion is congruent with the theory that, regardless of gender, people are engaged throughout life in a developmental dialectic between psychosocial experiences of intimacy with and autonomy from others (Shor & Sanville, 1978). The degree of emphasis placed on one or another of the dimensions of this dialectic will vary in association with culture, patterns of socialization, the stages of the life cycle, and other situational influences.

Perhaps gains from the women's movement and greater participation by men in child care will offer them more permission to express their proclivities for intimacy and nurturance and, thus, contribute more equitably to elder care. For this ideal to find expression in practice, however, continuing development of programs and policies that encourage men to participate fully in caregiving across the life span is imperative. Only with a high level of explicit public support will the optimism for change expressed by one of our respondents begin to be realized:

> Most women have raised children and have more practice in caring for someone. Today, however, if both husband and wife work, both spend equal time raising the kids. These men will then have had more of the experience of caring when they have to care for the elderly.

166   Male Elder Caregivers

References

Abel, E. K. (1990). Family care of the frail elderly. In E. K. Abel & M. K. Nelson (Eds.), *Circles of care: Work and identity in women's lives* (pp. 65-91). Albany: State University of New York Press.

Abel, E. K., & Nelson, M. K. (1990). Circles of care: An introductory essay. In E. K. Abel & M. K. Nelson (Eds.), *Circles of care: Work and identity in women's lives* (pp. 4-34). Albany: State University of New York Press.

Applegate, J. S. (1987). Beyond the dyad: Including the father in separation-individuation. *Child and Adolescent Social Work Journal, 4,* 92-105.

Baum, M., & Page, M. (1991). Caregiving and multigenerational families. *The Gerontologist, 31,* 762-769.

Bergman, S. J. (1991). Men's psychological development: A relational perspective. *Work in Progress,* Vol. 48. Wellesley, MA: Stone Center Working Paper Series.

Block, J. (1984). *Sex role identity and ego development.* San Francisco: Jossey-Bass.

Bould, F., Sanborn, B., & Reif, L. (1989). *Eighty-five plus: The oldest old.* Belmont, CA: Wadsworth.

Brody, E. M. (1986). Filial care of the elderly and changing roles of women (and men). *Journal of Geriatric Psychiatry, 19,* 175-201.

Cath, S. H., Gurwitt, A. R., & Ross, J. M. (Eds.). (1982). *Father and child: Developmental and clinical prespectives.* Boston: Little, Brown.

Chodorow, N. (1978). *The reproduction of mothering: Psychoanalysis and the sociology of gender.* Berkeley: University of California Press.

Davies, H., Priddy, J. M., & Tinklenberg, J. R. (1986). Support groups for male caregivers of Alzheimer's patients. *Clinical Gerontologist, 5,* 385-395.

Enright, R. B. (1991). Time spent caregiving and help received by spouses and adult children of brain-impaired adults. *The Gerontologist, 31,* 375-383.

Finley, N. J. (1989). Theories of family labor as applied to gender differences in caregiving for elderly parents. *Journal of Marriage and the Family, 51,* 79-86.

Fitting, M., Rabins, P., Lucas, M. J., & Eastham, J. (1986). Caregivers for dementia patients: A comparison of husbands and wives. *The Gerontologist, 26,* 248-252.

George, L. K. (1984). The burden of caregiving: How much? What kinds? For whom? *Center Reports on Advances in Caregiving, 8,* 1-8.

George, L. K., & Gwyther, L. P. (1986). Caregiver well-being: A multidimensional examination of family caregivers of demented adults. *The Gerontologist, 26,* 253-259.

Gilligan, C. (1982). *In a different voice.* Cambridge, MA: Harvard University Press.

Gregory, D. M., Peters, N., & Cameron, C. F. (1990). Elderly male spouses as caregivers: Toward an understanding of their experience. *Journal of Gerontological Nursing, 16,* 20-24.

Gutmann, D. (1987). *Reclaimed powers: Toward a new psychology of men and women in later life.* New York: Basic Books.

Horowitz, A. (1985). Sons and daughters as caregivers to older parents: Differences in role performance and consequences. *The Gerontologist, 25,* 612-617.

Kaye, L. W., & Applegate, J. S. (1990a). *Men as caregivers to the elderly: Understanding and aiding unrecognized family support.* Lexington, MA: Lexington Books.

Kaye, L. W., & Applegate, J. S. (1990b). Men as elder caregivers: A response to changing families. *American Journal of Orthopsychiatry, 60,* 86-95.

Liptzin, B. (1984). Discussion of "Elderly men as caregivers of wives." *Journal of Geriatric Psychiatry, 17*, 61-68.

Miller, B. (1990). Gender differences in spouse management of the care-giver role. In E. K. Abel & M. K. Nelson (Eds.), *Circles of care: Work and identity in women's lives* (pp. 92-104). Albany: State University of New York Press.

Motenko, A. K. (1988). Respite care and pride in caregiving: The experience of six older men caring for their disabled wives. In S. Reinharz & G. D. Rowles (Eds.), *Qualitative Gerontology* (pp. 104-127). New York: Springer.

Mothers bearing a second burden. (1989, May 14). *The New York Times*, p. 14.

Ory, M. G. (1985). The burden of care: A familial perspective. *Generations, 10*, 14-18.

Pruett, K. (1987). *The nurturing father.* New York: Warner Books.

Rathbone-McCuan, E., & Coward, R. T. (1985, November). *Male helpers: Unrecognized informal supports.* Paper presented at the 38th Annual Scientific Meeting of the Gerontological Society of America, New Orleans.

Schick, F. L. (1986). *Statistical handbook on aging Americans.* Phoenix: Onyx Press.

Sherman, S. R., Ward, R. A., & LaGory, M. (1988). Women as caregivers of elderly: Instrumental and expressive support. *Social Work, 33*, 164-161.

Shor, J., & Sanville, J. (1978). *Illusion in loving: A psychoanalytic approach to the evolution of intimacy and autonomy.* Los Angeles: Double Helix Press.

Siegel, J. S., & Taeuber, C. M. (1986). Demographic perspectives on the long-lived society. *Daedalus, 115*, 77-119.

Sommers, T. (1985). Caregiving: A woman's issue. *Generations, 10*, 9-13.

Stoller, E. P. (1983). Parent caregiving by adult children. *Journal of Marriage and the Family, 45*, 851-858.

Stoller, E. P. (1990). Males as helpers: The role of sons, relatives, and friends. *The Gerontologist, 30*, 228-235.

Sussman, M. B. (1985). The family life of old people. In R. H. Binstock & E. Shanas (Eds.), *Handbook of aging and the social sciences* (2nd. ed., pp. 415-449). New York: Van Nostrand Reinhold.

Wood, J. (1987). Labors of love. *Modern Maturity, 30*, 28-34.

Zarit, J. M. (1982). *Predictors of burden and distress for caregivers of senile dementia patients.* Unpublished doctoral dissertation, University of Southern California.

Zarit, S., Todd, P. A., & Zarit, J. M. (1986). Subjective burden of husbands and wives as caregivers: A longitudinal study. *The Gerontologist, 26*, 260-266.

10

Male Strippers

Men Objectifying Men

RICHARD TEWKSBURY

Definitions of masculinity have traditionally positioned men as sexual aggressors and objectifiers, not the pursued or the sexually objectified. Whereas women have frequently been judged by their attractiveness and seductiveness (Ronai & Ellis, 1989), this has been less common for men. Men who work as strippers represent a potential challenge to this social norm. This chapter examines the processes and consequences of sexual objectification of men in homosocial settings. In particular, I examine how the role of stripping is transformed when men are the ones who are sexually objectified by other men.

This study is based on 2 years' participant observation with five male strip groups. Four of the five troupes travel extensively through the Midwest and occasionally to Southern and East Coast cities. Performances are typically for male audiences, although all have performed for female audiences. Throughout the study period I periodically traveled with one troupe, conducting informal interviews and both structured and unstructured observations during dozens of shows. I also completed both structured and informal interviews with strippers (N = approximately 30), group managers and owners, nightclub managers, and men attending performances.

My research indicates that although male strippers occupy roles previously relegated to females, these roles are restructured to emphasize the traditionally masculine ideals of success, admiration, and respect. Male stripping integrates traditional elements of masculinity with the female-dominated occupational role, which enables men to maintain patriarchal privileges not available to female strippers. In effect, men exercise powers of "eminent domain," annexing and "improving" what was once the exclusive domain of women.

The dramaturgical perspective is a useful approach for analyzing the process and consequences of men supplanting women and subsequently masculinizing roles. This perspective is most closely associated with Erving Goffman, and has been insightfully employed to study exclusively male, closed interactional contexts by Delph (1978), Donnelly (1981), Humphreys (1970), Kamel (1983), McDermott and King (1988), Smith (1988), and Tewksbury (1990). The dramaturgical perspective takes as central the proposition that interaction is socially constructed and that actions (not individuals) are the foundation of meaning. Interactions are therefore the proper units of analysis for the study of social structure (Allen & Scheibe, 1982). Through interaction individuals construct and reconstruct meanings, creating their social contexts. When social action is seen as actively managed and constructed, the process whereby men appropriate and assimilate "female" roles while perpetuating definitions of masculinity is made clear.

Dramaturgical analysis makes theoretically central the fulfillment of roles analogous to those in theatrical performances. The production and management of social encounters—and maintenance of social institutions—rely on reciprocally dependent contributions from structurally defined roles. The roles most central in the organization of male stripping are those of stripper, playwright, director, producer, and audience. My discussion elaborates on these dramaturgical roles, focusing on how they both accommodate traditional role elements and incorporate male-centered perspectives in reshaping and reconstituting the performance of stripping.

Strippers

The central actors of the male strip show are the young men who remove their clothing while dancing in nightclubs. These men are neither wholly financially dependent upon, nor seeking to establish lasting careers in stripping. A majority of dancers interviewed for this project either attend college or work at white-collar/semiprofessional occupations by day. Chris, who was interviewed during his lunch break from a major corporation, explains his participation: "Why dance?

Well, I like the extra money and also the stimulation that it provides. Besides that, well, I guess you could say it just fills a need I feel right now." Similarly, Ben, a college graduate who has been stripping for more than 5 years, explains that while he doesn't foresee himself continuing as a stripper for very long, he has yet to find a job that pays as well as dancing:

> You get used to the quick money. . . . It's hard to explain. You don't want to come home and look for a job (when) last night you made $200. Why do you want to look in the paper for a job where you're going to make $5 an hour? You know, something's wrong! Why work for your money if you can do it dancing?

Few dancers drink, smoke, or use illegal drugs, and many are involved in stable relationships with significant others. A majority of dancers are gay; however, a sizable minority (30% to 40%) identify as exclusively heterosexual.

For heterosexually identified dancers, working in gay nightclubs is seen as simply one of the minor frustrations accompanying a high-paying job. There are, however, ways of finding positives within such frustrations. Ben recalls:

> (The manager) wanted me to do some gay bars, I said "hell, no!" Not "no," but "hell, no!" Eventually, though, I just saw how much money they were making, I thought well, when I need the money bad enough I'll probably do that. And that time came and I started doing it. I thought, what the heck, I need some money, I'll give it another shot. Plus, a lot of the bars are . . . like I've proven, there's a select few good-looking women, so that was enough incentive. . . . Plus my job at that point was getting sour. . . . I thought this would be fine until I get something together to get the job that I want. But I don't plan on doing this much longer, for men anyway.

Indeed, I observed that several dancers met and subsequently dated women who attend shows in gay nightclubs. Although it is not clear why these women are in gay nightclubs, the heterosexual dancers are clearly drawn to them to justify their performing for mostly male audiences.

The strippers' role is twofold, functioning as both antagonist and protagonist in the scripted drama. Dancers are the central protagonists in the interactions; they are the objects of audiences' attention and desire. Male strippers are complicit in their sexual objectification. The dancer tries to project an attractive personality, while emphasizing his sexual value. The importance of such an emphasis is explained by Frank, the manager of one highly successful troupe: "It's neat to be an individual, and it's neat to be your own person, but within that being your own person you have to be able to conform to what people expect to see."

Yet even as they entice and excite audience members, strippers avert attempts to consume them as sexual objects (Boles & Garbin, 1974; Ronai & Ellis, 1989). Dancers define their role as attracting, yet keeping distant, sexually aroused observers. As explained by one dancer:

> The guys, they want to pull open your T-strap and look and feel and grope and I find it really, really, really gross. It's offensive, I do, I hate it. But if they don't get out of hand, okay. I don't even mind if they look and I don't mind if they grab me gently, just kind of a touch, but when they start groping I let them know. Lately I've been telling them, "Hey, none of that shit!"

Few, if any, male strippers engage in sexual activities with audience members, and only in very rare instances is sex exchanged for money. This contrasts with much of the literature on female strippers, which suggests that prostitution is an occasional, if not common, way to supplement their incomes (Prus & Irini, 1980; Ronai & Ellis, 1989; Salutin, 1971; Skipper & McCaghy, 1970).

Most male strippers do not think very highly of the men in their audiences. Ben, a champion bodybuilder and popular male stripper, describes the men in his audiences as follows:

> Two words, this is great: eyeballs and hard-ons! Everybody's out there with eyeballs and hard-ons. . . . That summarizes it, they sit there and they're just, sometimes my favorite thing to do is to dance up to somebody and inevitably they're looking right at my crotch!

Such sentiments are near universal among strippers, both male and female (Boles & Garbin, 1974; Dressel & Petersen, 1982a; McCaghy & Skipper, 1969; Ronai & Ellis, 1989). Male dancers, like their female counterparts, complain that they are only bodies (or body parts), not persons, to their audiences. Audiences are described by male strippers as hypercritical, unpredictable, and "too cheap to tip." Audience members are also objects (dollar bills), at least in the eyes of dancers.

Because of their success in antagonizing audience members, questions arise regarding dancers' personal ethics and morality. Ben suggests that this is very frustrating for him:

> It really bothers me to think that I feel like I'm using them. It really does. I feel like a jerk when I go up to them and they're giving me money, stuffing money, being real nice to me, treating me kind and I don't have any interest in them.

This suggests, then, that some strippers are antagonistic not only toward those viewing and defining them as objects, but also toward themselves for casting themselves as unattainable ideals (i.e., "objects").

Many female strippers develop lesbian relationships with other strippers (McCaghy & Skipper, 1969; Salutin, 1971). While most of the male dancers in this study are gay, relationships with fellow dancers are extremely rare. In fact, one veteran of more than 3 years says that his troupe explicitly prohibits dating among the strippers, saying that the results would be a "nightmare" because individual dancers have "competition with everybody" and "there's always jealousy." Other troupes discourage relationships between dancers, and report that only rarely do such relationships develop. Two dancers, both working for the same troupe, explain:

> It's a small competition between everybody. You know, who can make the most tips or who can get the most out of a particular man.

> We're best of friends, but we're always trying to outdo each other. Always. It never fails that we try to outdo each other . . . see who can get the cutest guy, or see who can get the most tips.

Thus, male strippers differ from their female counterparts in three significant ways. Generally speaking, male strippers voluntarily elect to pursue this line of work, often in addition to other "real" jobs (Dressel & Petersen, 1982b). This contrasts directly with others' reports of female strippers (Carey, Peterson, & Sharpe, 1974; Prus & Irini, 1980; Ronai & Ellis, 1989; Skipper & McCaghy, 1970). Second, the male strippers in this study were not found to be engaged in prostitution, as has been previously reported for female strippers (Prus & Irini, 1980; Ronai & Ellis, 1989; Skipper & McCaghy, 1970) and men stripping for women (Dressel & Petersen, 1982a). These differences may be because male strippers have more economic opportunities outside stripping than women strippers. Third, although a majority of these male strippers are gay, their relationships are not with other dancers. In contrast, lesbian strippers are often involved in relationships with their colleagues (McCaghy & Skipper, 1969; Salutin, 1971). In general, female strippers are reported to develop strong friendships within their work groups, while male strippers are friendly yet very competitive with their colleagues.

Playwrights

Playwrights script performances. They define how the strippers will be sexually objectified. The playwright is the main creative force behind the images and dance moves presented on stage. Although dancers usually select their music, the playwright determines their costumes, order of performance, and participation in choreographed productions. The playwright is the initial creative force in producing an entertaining and desirable experience. One troupe manager explains the value of a troupe's creative director: "Whoever runs that group, or whoever gets involved in this business has got to be at least semicreative. You have to be constantly thinking of new and different things. . . . You need to come up with new and different things . . . they like to see creativity."

Here, in the area of creativity and image construction, is another clear example of how male stripping is significantly different from female stripping. Women who strip are molded into objects by manipulating their stylistic presentations, usually portraying exaggerated feminine stereotypes (Gonos, 1976; Robboy, 1985; Ronai & Ellis, 1989). However, for men the stripper role is infused with traditional masculine influences. The sexual images defined as desirable for men include muscular bodybuilders, athletes in macho sports (football, wrestling, baseball), and men of powerful and physically dominating status (soldiers, Indian chiefs, police officers, cowboys). Popular object images also include moderated versions of the macho image, such as the "pretty boys" rather than bodybuilders, athletes of noncontact sports (swimming, cycling, gymnastics), and men with status in social, rather than physical, power (business executives, rock musicians, doctors). Each of these images (with the exception of "the pretty boy") presents the stripper as a potentially dominant, and objectifying, object. Their power is linked to their physical prowess or occupational success—both traditional features of masculinity. In contrast, female sex objects are most commonly presented as passive, disempowered objects to be controlled by the objectifying consumer. When men are portrayed as sexual objects, they maintain power, dominance, and an ability to objectify others.

Furthermore, as increasing numbers of men gain ascendancy in the previously female-identified occupation of stripping, there comes an accompanying legitimation and "cleansing" of the stripper role. This is largely attributable to playwrights. One troupe manager (who directs all creative work for his troupe) believes male stripping will eventually be defined as socially normative and widely accepted: "I really wanted to . . . take it out of the dirty, sleazy mode and turn it into entertainment so you could take your grandmother in to see a show."

Perhaps this is an exaggeration (although several dancers have invited family members, including mothers and grandmothers, to shows), yet it demonstrates the mainstreaming intent of playwrights. The implication is that female stripping is "dirty" and "sleazy," while the sexual objectification of men is something better, something more socially normative, something to which "you could take your grandmother."

In the world of male stripping, the playwright fulfills the same general role that he would with female strippers, but the emphases within the role are modified. A female strip show script would be expected to play almost exclusively on exaggerated stereotypes of vulnerability; a male strip show script instead focuses on images of potential dominance. The fantasies created for a male strip show audience include images that are powerful, not merely objects available for the taking, as might be expected with female strippers.

Directors

The director is responsible for bringing the playwright's ideas to fruition, molding actors' performances to the playwright's ideas and the audience's expectations. The director is typically responsible for a troupe's business matters, as well as coordinating the playwright's artistic suggestions with the strippers' performances. In more established and commercially successful troupes, the director is not a dancer; but in less established troupes, dancers themselves share the director's responsibilities.

The director is also responsible for all personnel and training functions within a troupe. In this regard directors are charged with finding new recruits and molding them into consumable sexual objects. Frank oversees all personnel matters for his troupe, and recruits dancers by placing classified ads in community and university newspapers and by personally inviting men to audition. Frank has found dancers in grocery stores, at health clubs, walking on university campuses, in restaurants, and in audiences at his troupe's shows. Personally soliciting men is Frank's most efficient and productive means of finding dancers:

> I have better luck picking people out. I mean, if I go to a gym for instance, and I pick out, at least I get to see a naked body. . . . If I see them at a bar, I

at least get to see danceability and how they work in a crowd. But I don't necessarily see the bodies.

Directors function as mentors to new dancers, guiding them through exercises to better understand their sexuality and sensuality and consequently be better able to project and manage images as sexual objects. As one manager explains, "My thrust and my enjoyment comes out of training, interviewing, and creating these new people. Once they're out there dancing, then they're kind of on their own, and I try to guide and direct a little bit. But my job's over with them."

Directors train new dancers how to appear desirable while maintaining both an interpersonal and physical distance from audience members. Training sessions for new dancers typically begin with instructions on "defensive tipping" practices: controlling access to the body while accepting dollar bills either by hand or in the T-strap bikini. Controlling how and when audiences see and touch various parts of the body is crucial to being perceived as desirable yet not abused and sexy yet not vulgar. For one troupe, defensive tipping practices became important:

[A]fter dancing a little bar . . . where they wanted to see dick and nothing else. They [the audience] didn't care about anyone or anything, they just wanted to see dick. The guys could not dance; all they could do was take both hands, pull their straps up and hold them. . . . So defensive tipping is how to defend yourself without offending your audience. . . . When they come in here to train to be a stripper they're normally scared to death. . . . [Teaching them how to accept tips] makes them feel good about themselves, it makes them feel a little bit more like a stripper, like they're getting into the meat of what's going to happen to them.

In essence, the director teaches the strippers how to dominate and control the interactions with the audience.

While only men who are physically attractive are hired as strippers, many lack basic dance and performance skills. It is the director's charge to teach these skills to the dancers, thereby creating objects that are desirable—physically, sexually, and personally—to other men. Success for a male stripper, from the director's point of view, hinges upon:

[F]our elements . . . there's looks, there's body, danceability, and personality. . . . You need to have at least two to work. You can be ugly as a mud fence, have a terrific body and a terrific personality, and they'll love you to death.

Or, you can have a pretty face and an ugly body and a terrific personality, and they'll love you. Or there are other combinations, too.

Dancers' physical bodies can be modified, but only within limits, so directors focus on dance style and presentation of personality.

In addition to training dancers and blending them with the playwright's vision, the director handles the business dealings of the group. A director's responsibilities include providing and coordinating necessary costumes and props, and providing transportation and overnight accommodations for out-of-town performances. Directors also negotiate bookings and appearance fees with nightclubs and act as bookkeeper and payroll officer, dispensing salaries to individual dancers. Troupe members typically do not share equally in a troupe's appearance fee. Rather, more experienced and more celebrated dancers receive larger salaries. Incomes also vary across individual dancers because of differences in individually collected tips. Directors receive the greatest share of the company's profits. It is standard for 50% of all receivables to go to the director. Dancers are only marginally involved in a troupe's business dealings; most dancers have minimal knowledge about their troupe's financial status. More often than not troupes operate on minimal budgets, being only marginally successful business enterprises.

Producers

The producers of male strip shows are the individuals or organizations who financially support troupes. Producers control whether troupes will be provided bookings, thereby controlling troupes' opportunities to make money. Producers, the managers/owners of nightclubs, have the ultimate say in whether troupes perform, as well as in determining acceptable performance styles. Hence, by controlling the style, content, and financial inputs to troupes, producers can manipulate both troupes' and individuals' income potential. Whereas directors are troupe patriarchs, producers are the gatekeepers who decide whether troupes have access to paying audiences.

Producers are generally not involved in troupes' everyday activities, yet they are critical players because of their monetary resources. Occupants of the producer role are most commonly owners and managers of nightclubs. Because nightclubs can ban troupes (or individuals), their decrees and wishes are given highest priority by actors, playwrights, and directors. In contrast, in the world of female stripping, the producer role is combined with that of director, personified by owners of the clubs where strippers regularly perform. Because male strip troupes typically are not housed within one particular nightclub, these roles are distinct. In effect, the structure of the male stripping business incorporates an additional set of roles and players. These function to decentralize power. In male stripping more men are involved, hence power is more diffuse, though by no means equally shared.

Producers, however, do not share consensus regarding how the stripping business does or should operate, or what constitutes acceptable and desirable conduct. In fact, there tends to be widespread variation in what is considered appropriate, and profitable, interaction. One troupe director claims that:

> Every bar has their own set of rules and regulations. Even though the state may say this is the way it is, some bars may abide by those laws, some may say, "Who cares? Do what you want to do." Other bars have interpreted the [laws] in a different way.

While many troupes prefer nightclubs with a "who cares?" attitude, such nightclubs are the exception. Nightclub owners place top priority on their own business and freely and openly exert control over troupes in efforts to protect their financial interests and their reputations. If troupes, or individual dancers, are unwilling or unable to abide by such restrictions (e.g., arriving at least one hour before and starting within 10 minutes of advertised show times, limiting number of drinks consumed, meeting particular members of the staff or their guests, not mixing with audience members in certain areas of the nightclub), they will be left without financial support, without a place to perform, and therefore without an audience. One troupe manager, acknowledging the importance of cooperating with nightclubs, points out that this is a mutually beneficial relationship: "I know that we need the bar, we need the bar to be able to get in there and perform. But without us those bars will go right down the old poop-chute! So we have to work together."

Audience

Playwrights complain they must restrain their creativity because audiences are unsophisticated. Directors complain that playwrights expect too much abstract interpretation from an audience. Producers complain that audiences spend too much money tipping dancers and not enough purchasing drinks. Strippers complain that audience members are rude, cheap, and disrespectful. Even audience members complain (but usually only to friends or by throwing glares and stares) about audience members who use large tips to monopolize particular dancers' attentions.

But, no performance is complete without an audience. A typical audience for a male strip show will consist of between 100 and 500 persons, approximately 95% men, who arrive in groups of 3 or 4 or by themselves. Most nightclubs that host male strip shows do so on a regular basis, providing patrons with a predictable social outlet on a particular night of the week. Many patrons regularly attend, either arriving with or rendezvousing with friends. Apparently, for some members of the gay community, attendance is an routine part of social life.

As already discussed, a male strip show is not designed to facilitate interpersonal interactions between patrons and dancers. In this respect male strip shows differ somewhat from female strip shows, where interactions with customers are a central component of the stripper role (Boles & Garbin, 1974; Prus & Irini, 1980; Ronai & Ellis, 1989). Male strippers typically interact with audience members only in brief and highly focused fashions. Verbal exchanges are typically brief, and occur during a dancer's performance. Interactions primarily center on patrons approaching dancers to present them with tips.

The production of an entertaining experience is what male strip troupes seek to create for their audiences. When audience members enjoy themselves and enthusiasticly respond to performances, dancers are likely to interact in increasingly intimate manners with an audience—spending longer periods of time with individuals, reappearing in the nightclub audience after performing, or even thanking tippers with a kiss on the cheek—subsequently facilitating a greater flow of money from audience members to dancers. Audience members, via their applause, cheers, and of course, tips, have significant influence on the style and content of male strip shows. Most telling, and admittedly an extreme example, is a story related by one troupe of a former dancer who: "If the crowd was dead, he didn't take off his clothes. That's exactly how he was. I mean, he was the prick of pricks of dancers. But if the crowd wasn't making any noise, he wouldn't take off his clothes."

Dancers perform to make money; their actions and interactions are designed to maximize their income. Audiences therefore control dancers' activities insofar as they ultimately control the purse strings. Control, however, is exerted both ways. Men in the audience have something dancers want: money. Dancers possess and display qualities audience members are seeking: physical attractiveness and sexual access/fantasies. It is up to the individuals involved to negotiate their demands: How much money will obtain how much and what variety of object consumption?

Thus men do not directly control other men's sexuality in the same way they control women's sexuality. When interacting with female strippers, men do not negotiate with them for sexual access. Access to the female stripper is controlled by other men. Men's negotiations for access to a woman's sexuality are primarily to make interactions smoother and perhaps more entertaining. While female strippers do attach monetary prices to sexual access—paying for table dances or "private show-ings"—these negotiations are structured and maintained by men. Male club owners direct (and make economically necessary) the limits of women's exchanges. Hence, one group of men controls the sexual access opportunities of other men. Women, as a social category and as individuals, do not hold ultimate control of their sexuality. Sexual access to male strippers, though, *must* be obtained through negotiations with the individual. Each male stripper controls access to his body. The structure of male stripping does not require men to share their tips, nor to grant access to those they do not personally select. The consumption of male sexual objects, then, is characterized by modifying traditional patriarchal privileges within the arena of sexual objectification and consumption. Men control sexual access to themselves and to women.

Conclusion

Men modify interactional norms and status expectations when they occupy traditionally female occupational roles. Not only is the occupa-tional structure itself reconfigured, but the interactions of those within the occupation are also altered.

When men cross over, traditionally female occupational roles are modi-fied by incorporating traditional masculine ideals and sociostructural ele-ments of patriarchal privilege. In the case of male strippers, roles in which women may be viewed as deviant and sexually available are "cleansed" and presented in more economically oriented, rather than sexual, terms. The role of stripper is masculinized, hence made socially acceptable for men. This masculinization of roles is in part necessitated by the lack of roles in which men have experience as sexually objectified commodities. Such objects are known, to men, only as female roles. In order to both maintain a masculine identity and be constructed as a sexual object, it is necessary to restructure the role of sexual object. The role is injected with traditionally masculine influences, thereby mediating the potentially feminizing (i.e., demasculinizing) impact on dancers' identities.

When men annex roles from women, it is the roles, not the actors, that are modified. Roles are molded to correspond with men's conceptions of the role. Modifications center on contexts and interactions in which the individual participates. This suggests that as definitions of masculinity expand, it is actually the structure of interactional contexts, not the definitions of masculinity per se, that are reconstituted to facilitate occupation by masculine-identified actors. Crossing over, then, is not a process of men moving to "female" occupations, but rather men drawing occupations to their present location within patriarchal social structures. Crossing over, in the case of male strippers, is a reconfiguration of social and occupational structures that maintain men's privileged social status.

References

Allen, V. L., & Scheibe, K. E. (1982). *The social context of conduct.* New York: Praeger.

Boles, J., & Garbin, A. (1974). The strip club and stripper-customer patterns of interaction. *Sociology and Social Research, 58,* 136-144.

Carey, S. H., Peterson, R. A., & Sharpe, L. K. (1974). A study of recruitment and socialization in two deviant female occupations. *Sociological Symposium, 11,* 11-24.

Delph, E. (1978). *The silent community: Public homosexual encounters.* Beverly Hills, CA: Sage.

Donnelly, P. (1981). Running the gauntlet: The moral order of pornographic movie theaters. *Urban Life, 10*(3), 239-264.

Dressel, P. L., & Petersen, D. M. (1982a). Gender roles, sexuality and the male strip show: The structuring of sexual opportunity. *Sociological Focus, 15*(2), 151-162.

Dressel, P. L., & Petersen, D. M. (1982b). Becoming a male stripper. *Work and Occupations, 9*(3), 387-406.

Gonos, G. (1976). Go-go dancing: A comparative frame analysis. *Urban Life, 9,* 189-219.

Humphreys, L. (1970). *Tearoom trade: Impersonal sex in public places.* New York: Aldine.

Kamel, G. W. L. (1983). *Downtown street hustlers: The role of dramaturgical imaging practices in the social construction of male prostitution.* Unpublished doctoral dissertation, University of California, San Diego.

McCaghy, C., & Skipper, J. K. (1969, Fall). Lesbian behavior as an adaptation to the occupation of stripping. *Social Problems, 17,* 262-270.

McDermott, K., & King, R. D. (1988). Mind games: Where the action is in prisons. *British Journal of Criminology, 28*(3), 357-377.

Prus, R., & Irini, S. (1980). *Hookers, rounders & desk clerks.* Salem, WI: Sheffield.

Robboy, H. (1985). *Emotional labor and sexual exploitation in an occupational role.* Paper presented at the annual meetings of the MidSouth Sociological Society, Little Rock, AR.

Ronai, C. R., & Ellis, C. (1989). Turn-ons for money: Interactional strategies of the table dancer. *Journal of Contemporary Ethnography, 18*(3), 271-298.

Salutin, M. (1971). Stripper morality. *Trans-Action, 8,* 12-22.

Skipper, J. K., Jr., & McCaghy, C. (1970). Stripteasers: The anatomy and career contingencies of a deviant occupation. *Social Problems, 17*(3), 391-405.

Smith, N. E. (1988). *Impression management in the prison.* Unpublished doctoral dissertation, The Ohio State University.

Tewksbury, R. (1990). Patrons of porn: Research notes on the clientele of adult bookstores. *Deviant Behavior, 11*(3), 259-271.

Author Index

Subject Index

About the Contributors

Jim Allan teaches courses in social issues and the social foundations of education at the Tri-College Department of Education in Dubuque, Iowa. His chapter on male elementary teachers in this volume is part of a larger study examining these men's work and home lives, their career paths, the divisions of labor in teaching with women, and the effects on children of a "hidden curriculum" in which "women teach and men manage."

Jeffrey S. Applegate is an associate professor at the graduate school of social work and social research, Bryn Mawr College, where he teaches courses in developmental theory and clinical practice. A co-author of *Men as Caregivers to the Elderly: Understanding and Aiding Unrecognized Family Support*, Dr. Applegate has published numerous journal articles on changes in men's roles as caregivers across the life cycle. He has also researched and written about the application of developmental theory to clinical social work practice and is a consulting editor for the *Child and Adolescent Social Work Journal*.

Harriet Bradley is senior lecturer in sociology at the University of Sunderland. Her publications include *Men's Work, Women's Work*, a history of the sexual division of labor in Great Britain. She is currently working on an ESRC-funded research project on gender differentiation in trade unions.

Paula England is professor of sociology at the University of Arizona. Her interests include occupational sex segregation, the sex gap in pay, labor markets, and integrating sociological, economic, and feminist theories. She is author of *Comparable Worth: Theories and Evidence* and editor of *Theory on Gender/Feminism on Theory*. She will be editor of the *American Sociological Review* during 1993-1996. She has also served as an expert witness in federal litigation involving employment discrimination.

Melissa S. Herbert is a doctoral candidate in sociology at the University of Arizona. Her research interests include gender and labor markets, women and the military, and the social construction of sexuality. Her current research examines the coping strategies employed by women in the military. During 1993-1994, she will be student editorial assistant for the *American Sociological Review*.

Jerry A. Jacobs is an associate professor of sociology and chair of the graduate program in sociology at the University of Pennsylvania. His research has focused on the sex segregation of occupations and its intersection with career patterns. Recent projects include a study of women's entry into management and an analysis of trends in sex segregation in 56 countries. He has also edited a special issue of the sociology journal *Work and Occupations*, devoted to questions of sex segregation and gender stratification. In progress is a comparative study of women's employment in the public sector in 10 countries.

Kaisa Kauppinen-Toropainen is a senior research scientist at the Institute of Occupational Health, Helsinki, Finland. For the academic years 1987-1989, she was a visiting scholar at the University of Michigan in Ann Arbor. She has a Ph.D. in social psychology from the University of Helsinki, where she now holds a docent (associate professor) position. Her research covers gender roles, family, and work. She has written extensively on women's positions in the labor market in a cross-cultural perspective, having gathered data from the United States, the former Soviet Union, Estonia, and the Nordic countries. Her most recent article, for the International Labor Organization, was titled "Women in Nontraditional Occupations—International Comparisons: Impacts on the Quality of Work, Job Satisfaction, and Stress." She is editor of a forthcoming book, *Unresolved Dilemmas: Women, Work, and Family in the United States, Europe and the Soviet Union.*

Lenard W. Kaye is a professor at Bryn Mawr College graduate school of social work and social research. He is the author of *Home Health Care*, co-author of *Resolving Grievances in the Nursing Home* and *Men as Caregivers to the Elderly*, and co-editor of *Congregate Housing for the Elderly*. He has published more than 60 book chapters and journal articles on issues in elder caregiving, long-term care advocacy, adult day care, home healthcare, retirement life-styles, and social work curriculum development. His current research is in the areas of self-help support groups for older women, and the ethical and legal aspects of high-technology home care.

Johanna Lammi has studied sociology at the University of Helsinki. She graduated in 1990 and is currently returning to her studies after maternity leave.

Rosemary Pringle is an associate professor of sociology at Macquarie University in Sydney, Australia, where she is also chair of the women's studies committee. She is author of *Secretaries Talk: Sexuality, Power and Work*, co-author of *Gender at Work*, and has published numerous papers on sexuality, work, and the state. Her current research interests include gender and the professions, and a series of concrete studies of the body, which have led her to reflect on the place of female butchers and funeral directors. She is currently writing a book about women in medicine, which will combine all of these interests.

Richard Tewksbury is an assistant professor in the school of justice administration at the University of Louisville, Kentucky. His research focuses on deviance and the social construction of gender in marginalized populations. His work has appeared in *Deviant Behavior, American Journal of Criminal Justice*, and the *Journal of Criminal Justice Education*. Currently, he is working on dramaturgically guided investigations of the lives of persons living with HIV/AIDS.

Wayne J. Villemez is a professor and head of the sociology department at the University of Connecticut. He has published widely in the area of inequality, with a particular focus both on organization/stratification linkages, and on racial and gender inequality.

Christine L. Williams is an assistant professor of sociology at The University of Texas-Austin. She is the author of *Gender Differences at*

Work, a study of male nurses and female marines. She is completing a new book on the status of men in nursing, elementary school teaching, librarianship, and social work.

L. Susan Williams is a doctoral student in sociology currently studying with Wayne J. Villemez at the University of Connecticut. She specializes in stratification and political sociology.